THE FAITH REQUIRED TO GET TO HEAVEN

G. Michael Cocoris

Table Of Contents

Preface   1
Introduction
Chapter 1   Various Views of Faith   5

Faith is Mental Assent to a Proposition   5
Faith is Belief in a Promise   7
Faith is Trust   8
Faith is Mental, Emotional, and Volitional   10
Faith is Commitment   11

Chapter 2   The Biblical Explanation of Faith   15

The Definition of Faith   15
The Content of Faith   20
The Nature of Faith   31

Chapter 3   The Conversion of Famous Christians   35

Augustine   35
Martin Luther   37
John Calvin   38
John Wesley   39
Charles Haddon Spurgeon   41
R. A. Torrey   44

Chapter 4   Conclusion   47

Various Views of Faith   47
The Biblical Explanation   50
Testimonies   51

Appendix: GES View of The Saving Message   57

My Connection   58
The Changes   60
The Corrections   67

Bibliography   80
About The Author   85

PREFACE

What must one do to go to heaven? Shortly after my conversion, I was taught to tell people, "Ask Jesus to come into your heart" (Rev. 3:20). I did that for a while. Then, I began training others using the "ask Jesus to come into your heart" model. But when I listened to someone I had trained use Revelation 3:20 to lead a teenager to Christ, it was apparent that the teenager did not get saved. He prayed the prayer, but based on what he said afterward, it was evident he did not get saved.

That experience prompted me to investigate Revelation 3:20. I concluded that it is not a salvation verse. For one thing, it does not say "into" (one word); it says "in to" (two words). Jesus is not saying He would come <u>into</u> a person. He says that if someone opened the door of a building, He would come <u>in</u> <u>to</u> be with that individual. Furthermore, Jesus did not say He would save such a person. He said He would dine with that individual, which means they would have fellowship together. Revolution 3:20 is not about salvation; It is about fellowship. So, I stopped using Revelation 3:20 to lead people to Christ.

Then, I began using Romans 10:13 to lead people to the Lord. It says, "For whoever calls on the name of the Lord shall be saved." At that point, I was a sophomore in college. I had been a believer for two years.

As I recall, for the rest of my college days and during my years in seminary, I continued to use Romans 10:13 as a verse to lead people to Christ. At the end of my gospel presentation, I invited people to pray. My suggested prayer was, "God, I admit I have sinned. I believe Jesus died for my sin, and I want to trust Him to save me right now."

I am not sure when, but I think it was after I graduated from seminary that I realized Romans 10:13 is not an evangelistic verse either! The context of Romans 10:13 and the content of Romans 10:13-14 convince me of that.

The context of Romans 10:13 begins with Romans 10:9: "If you confess with your mouth the Lord Jesus and believe in your heart that God has raised Him from the dead, you will be saved." The issue is the word "saved." The Greek word translated "saved" means "delivered." It is used to describe being delivered from danger, disease, and physical death, as well as being spiritually delivered. Moreover, when used of spiritual salvation, it can either be "I have been saved" (Eph. 2:8), "I am being saved" (1 Cor. 1:18), or "I will be saved (Heb. 9:27-28). In other words, spiritual salvation is from the penalty of sin (past tense), from the power of sin (present tense), and from the presence of sin (future tense).

In Romans, Paul distinguishes between being justified and being saved, suggesting he uses "save" in the sense of being saved from the power of sin. In Romans 5:9, Paul states, "Much more then, having now been justified by His blood, we shall be saved from wrath through Him." He explains in the next verse, "For if when we were enemies, we were reconciled to God through the death of His Son, much more, having been reconciled, we shall be saved by His life" (Rom. 5:10). "Being saved by his life" is a reference to being saved from the power of sin (Rom. 6:4).

That same distinction is in Romans 10. Romans 10:9 speaks of confessing with the mouth and believing in the heart. In verse 10, Paul explains that ("for") when he says, "For with the heart one believes unto righteousness, and with the mouth confession is made unto salvation." Clearly, faith produces righteousness, that is, justification, and confession with the mouth produces salvation, which in Romans is being saved from the power of sin.

The content of Romans 10:13-14 indicates that those verses are not an evangelistic passage. When Romans 10:13 says, "For whoever calls on the name of the Lord shall be saved," it is not referring to justification ("I have been saved"); it speaks to the spiritual life ("I am being saved"). That is evident not only in Romans 10:9-10 but also in Romans 10:13-14. Those two verses say, "For whoever calls on the name of the Lord shall be saved. How then shall they call on Him in whom they have not believed? And how shall they believe in Him of whom they have not heard? And how shall they hear without a preacher?"

In other words, to be saved from the power of sin, one must have a preacher, hear the message, believe in the Lord (at that point one is declared righteous, Rom. 10:10), and call on the Lord (confess with the mouth, Rom. 10:9-10). To say the same thing another way, in Romans 10, justification (being saved from the *penalty* of sin) is by faith (Rom. 10:10), and being saved from the *power* of sin is by confession with the mouth (Rom. 10:10), that is, by calling on the Lord (Rom. 10:13).

At any rate, by the time I was teaching evangelism at Dallas Seminary in 1974, I was teaching students to conclude their gospel presentation with Ephesians 2:8-9.

In my preaching and gospel presentations to individuals, I also emphasized the need to trust Christ and His finished work on the cross. Haddon Robinson, my mentor, pointed out that the New Testament says to trust Jesus Christ, a person, not a doctrine of the atonement. As a result of that conversation, I began saying, "Trust Jesus Christ, who died for your sins and rose from the dead." For decades, my evangelistic message in personal conversations, in preaching, and in print has been to trust Jesus Christ, who died for your sins and rose from the dead.

Somewhere along the line (I think it was in the mid-80s), I talked with Zane Hodges about saving faith. I remember walking away from that conversation, thinking that one of the best ways to explain conversion is "I saw the light" (2 Cor. 4:4). That realization affected how I presented the gospel to individuals. In my presentation, I explained that we are sinners, that the penalty of sin is death, that Jesus died to pay the penalty for our sins, and, therefore, the penalty of our sins is completely paid for, and there was nothing we could do to add to that. I was looking for that ah-ha moment. I wanted to hear the person I was speaking to say something like, "Oh, I see!" Usually, even if I hear that, I would still have the person pray, although not always.

The next time I grappled with saving faith was about 2007. Jack Moulton, a friend who is now with the Lord, informed me that Zane Hodges had written two articles on how to lead people to Christ, in which he said that all that was necessary for people to be saved was that they believe that Jesus was the guarantor of eternal life. Jack and I spent hours on the phone (he lived in Phoenix and I was in Santa Monica), discussing Zane's new view. As a result of those conversations, when I wrote the book *The Salvation Controversy* (dedicated to my friend Jack), I said the issue was not the minimum that people had to believe to be saved; the issue is we are commanded to preach the gospel, meaning that Jesus died to pay for sin and rose from the dead (Cocoris, *The Salvation Controversy*, 2008/2024 edition, p. 20).

After that, I did not think about saving faith again until 2018. After reading several GES blogs that mentioned saving faith, I began discussing the nature of saving faith with Kerry Fager, a young man who had asked me to mentor him. As a result of those discussions, I decided to write a paper on saving faith, not for publication but to help me think through the subject. J. N. Darby, whose published works number over 40 volumes of 600 pages each, once said to William Kelly, another author, "You write to be read and understood; I only think on paper" (Bass, pp. 58, 61). Much of what I have written has been simply a way to use pen and paper to help me think through ideas. So, I wrote about saving faith. This book is an expanded version of that paper.

After finishing the paper on saving faith, I sent it to three selected friends. Before they could even open the email I sent, I decided to read one more book on the subject of saving faith: Thomas L. Stegall's *The Gospel of Christ: A Biblical Response to the Crossless Gospel Regarding the Contents of Saving Faith*

(2009). He had sent me a copy because he quoted me in it. When I first received it, I promptly put it on my bookshelf without reading it. I had made up my mind about the content of saving faith and did not want to take the time to read his 826-page tome on the subject.

One of the reasons I decided to read Tom's book was that my wife, Patricia, and I took a trip to Hawaii. I knew I had a five-hour flight going and a five-hour flight coming back, so I would have time to read. I did not want to start studying any other new subjects on my list, so, at the last minute, I tossed Tom's book in my luggage and thought I would leisurely peruse some of it. Since I thought I already knew what he would say, I thought this would be more casual reading than serious study.

Boy, was I surprised! Tom did extensive (exhausting) research concerning the Grace Evangelical Society's (GES) view of the content of saving faith (his "Bibliography of Works Cited" is 31 pages long). Although I was generally familiar with the topics Tom wrote about, I gained a much deeper understanding from his book. So, wanting to think through the GES view, I decided to write a paper. That material is also included in this book. See the appendix.

Writing all of this has helped me think through the subject of faith when leading people to the Lord. I trust it will help you do the same thing.

G. Michael Cocoris
Santa Monica, CA

Introduction

Among those who believe that salvation is by grace through faith, there are different opinions regarding the meaning of faith. Since salvation is by faith, it is of the utmost importance that the correct meaning of faith is understood. What is the meaning of the faith required to get to heaven?

By Faith Let's start with the most fundamental issue: salvation is by faith, not by works. That is two sides of the same coin. First, salvation is by faith. "For God so loved the world that He gave His only begotten Son, that whoever believes in Him should not perish but have everlasting life" (Jn. 3:16). "He who believes in the Son has everlasting life; and he who does not believe the Son shall not see life, but the wrath of God abides on him" (Jn. 3:36). "Most assuredly, I say to you, he who believes in Me has everlasting life" (Jn. 6:47). "So they said, 'Believe on the Lord Jesus Christ, and you will be saved, you and your household'" (Acts. 16:31).

Not by Works Second, salvation is not by works. "For by grace you have been saved through faith, and that not of yourselves; it is the gift of God, not of works, lest anyone should boast" (Eph. 2:8-9). "For if Abraham was justified by works, he has something to boast about, but not before God. For what does the Scripture say? 'Abraham believed God, and it was accounted to him for righteousness.' Now to him who works, the wages are not counted as grace but as debt. But to him who does not work but believes on Him who justifies the ungodly, his faith is accounted for righteousness" (Rom. 4:2-5). "Not by works of righteousness which we have done, but according to His mercy He saved us" (Titus 3:5).

Thus, the Scripture is clear: salvation is by faith, not by works. The two cannot be mixed. "And if by grace, then it is no longer of works; otherwise grace is no longer grace. But if it is of works, it is no longer grace; otherwise, work is no longer work" (Rom. 11:6). In other words, salvation is by faith *alone* and since the object of the faith in salvation by faith is only in Jesus Christ, salvation is by *faith alone in Christ alone*. "To say that we are justified by faith is just another way of saying that we are justified not in the slightest measured by ourselves, but simply and solely by the One in whom our faith is repose" (Machen, p. 172).

Some object to the idea that salvation is by faith alone. They point to James 2:24, which says, "Justification is by works and not by faith only." In the first place, James 2 teaches justification by faith: "And the Scripture was fulfilled which says, 'Abraham believed God, and it was accounted to him for righteousness.' And he was called the friend of God" (Jas. 2:23). So why does James say that justification is by works? Justification is by faith before *God*. Justification by works is before *people*. In Romans 4:2, Paul says, "If Abraham was justified by works, he has something to boast about, but not before God." Salvation before God is by faith alone in Christ alone, but to convince people that you have trusted Christ, you have to demonstrate that by works, which in the context of James 2 is loving people.

The Problem There are two problems with saying that salvation is by faith alone in Christ alone. In the first place, what is the meaning of faith? Among those who believe that salvation is by grace through faith, there are different views about the meaning of the faith required for getting to heaven. Those views will be explained in the next chapter.

The second problem is the meaning of Christ. Salvation is by faith alone, but faith itself does not save. Jesus saves. Faith is merely the means by which Jesus saves. To say the same thing another way, the Bible does not teach that people are saved *on account of* their faith but rather that they are saved *through* faith. In other words, the saving power resides not in the act of faith, nor in the nature of faith, but exclusively in the object of faith, Jesus Christ. The problem is, how much must one know about Christ to be saved? Among those who believe that salvation is by grace through faith, there is even a disagreement on that subject! To be saved, must one know about the virgin birth of Jesus? His sinless life? His death for sin? His resurrection from the dead? His Second Coming? His kingdom? Must one believe in His promise? His promise of what? His promise of assurance of salvation? His promise of eternal security?

Summary: The two problems related to salvation being by faith alone in Christ alone are the definition of faith and what a person needs to know about Christ.

Chapter 1

Various Views of Faith

Even among those who believe that salvation is by faith alone in Christ alone, there are various views about exactly what is involved. There are different explanations of the definition of faith and of what one must believe to get to heaven.

Faith is Mental Assent to a Proposition

Although early Christian writers spoke about faith, most did not define it. Some early theologians, however, did. They taught that faith is an intellectual belief. Augustine says, "To believe is nothing more than to think with assent" (Augustine, *On the Predestination of the Saints*, Book 1, Chapter 2). For Thomas Aquinas, faith is an assent to an understood proposition (Aquinas, *Summa Theologiae*, Second Part of the Second Part, Question 1, Article 2).

Gordon Clark Gordon H. Clark, a Christian philosophy professor, says, "Faith, by definition, is assent to understood propositions.... All saving faith is assent to one or more biblical propositions" (Clark, p. 118). Clark contends that the difference between various beliefs lies in the object or propositions believed, not in the nature of belief (Clark, p. 15). He says that the Greek verb "believe" means just that—"believe," period (Clark, p. 98).

Clark summarizes Kittel as saying, "To believe *in* is equivalent to believe *that*. To believe in Christ Jesus simply means to believe that Jesus died and rose again. And for John especially *to believe in* and *to believe that* are constantly used interchangeably" (Kittel vol. VI, pp. 203-208, cited by Clark, p. 101, italics his).

John Robbins, who wrote the Foreword of Clark's book, says Clark asserts that "faith is assent to a proposition, and that saving faith is assent to a proposition found in the Bible" (Robbins, in Clark, p. vii). Robbins even says that "trust in a person" is meaningless unless it means assenting to certain propositions about a person (Clark, p. vi). Clark says, "Even in English, when we say we believe a person, we mean we agree that his statement is true" (Clark, p. 98). Clark argues that the difference between various beliefs "lies in the objects or propositions believed, not in the nature of belief" (Clark, p. 15). He says, "Belief is the act of assenting to something understood. But understanding alone is not belief in what is understood" (Clark, p. 51).

So, if, in Clark's view, saving faith is giving assent to a proposition, what is the proposition? Clark's answer is, "There seems to be no other conclusion but that God justifies sinners by means of many combinations of propositions believed. For this reason, a minister should not confine himself to topics popularly thought to be 'evangelistic' but should preach the whole counsel of God, trusting that God will give someone the gift of faith through the sermons on the Trinity, eschatology, or the doctrine of immediate imputation" (Clark, p. 110). As a Calvinist, Clark believed that God gives people faith. So, in his view, ministers are to preach the Bible, and in the process God will give the elect faith. That is carrying the Calvinistic doctrine of God giving faith to an absurd extreme!

Faith is Belief in a Promise

Reformers Clark claims that the reformers "defined faith as an assent to the promise of the gospel" (Clark, p. 50). Calvin's definition of faith is: "a firm and certain knowledge of God's benevolence toward us, founded upon the truth of the freely given promise in Christ, both revealed to our minds and sealed upon our hearts through the Holy Spirit" (Calvin, *Institutes*, III, ii, 7). In his commentary on John 3:33, Calvin states, "To believe the gospel is nothing else than to assent to the truth which God has revealed."

Zane Hodges Clark's definition of saving faith influenced Zane Hodges. I know that because, in the 1980s, in discussing the nature of faith with him, he gave me a copy of Clark's book *Faith and Saving Faith*, complete with a note to me over his signature. However, Hodges would not use the term "mental assent." Nor did he accept Clark's view concerning the content of saving faith (assent to some proposition found in the Bible).

In his book *Absolutely Free* (henceforth *AF*), Zane Hodges says that faith is "the *inward conviction* that what God says to us in the gospel is true. That—and that alone—is saving faith" (Hodges, *AF*, p. 31, italics his) and "Faith, then, is taking God at

His Word. Saving faith is taking God at His Word in the gospel" (Hodges, *AF*, p. 32).

Later, Hodges changed his mind about what a person had to believe. Instead of faith taking God at His word *in the gospel*, he concluded that faith was believing that Jesus was the guarantor of eternal life.

Grace Evangelical Society (GES) When Zane Hodges was a Greek professor at Dallas Seminary, Bob Wilkin was one of his students. Bob Wilkin founded the Grace Evangelical Society. For a more detailed explanation of the GES view, see the appendix.

Faith is Trust

Thomas Manton Clark seems to suggest that Thomas Manton, a 17th-century Puritan (1620-1677) and clerk to the Westminster Assembly that produced the Larger Catechism, was the one who introduced the element of trust. In his commentary on James, Manton separates belief into three parts: *notitia, assensus, and fiducia*, that is, understanding, assent, and trust. Manton says, "It was the mistake of the former age [the age of the reformers] to make the promise, rather than the person of Christ, to be the formal object of faith" (Clark, p. 49).

Westminster Catechism Question 72 in the Larger Catechism (1647) says, "Justifying faith is a saving grace, wrought in the heart of the sinner, by the Spirit and the word of God, whereby he, being convicted of his sin and misery, and of the disability in himself and all other creatures to recover him out of his lost condition, not only assenteth to the truth of the promise of the gospel, but receives it and rest upon Christ and His righteousness therein set forth, for the pardon of sin, and for acceptance and accounting of his personal righteousness in the sight of God unto salvation." The phrase "rest upon Christ" expresses more the idea of trust than assent.

Charles Hodge In his commentary on Romans, Charles Hodge, the famous Reformed theologian, said: "That faith, therefore, which is connected with salvation, includes knowledge, that is, a perception of the truth and its qualities; accent, or the persuasion of the truth of the object of faith; and trust or reliance. The exercise, or state of mind expressed by the word faith, as used in the Scripture, is not mere mental assent or mere trust; it is the intelligent perception, reception, and reliance on the truth as revealed in the gospel" (Hodge, p. 29).

Charles Ryrie In his *Basic Theology* (hereafter, *BT*), Ryrie says, "Faith means confidence, trust, to hold something is true. Of course, faith must have content; there must be confidence or trust about something. To have faith in Christ unto salvation means to have confidence that He can remove the guilt of sin and grant eternal life" (Ryrie, *BT*, p. 326). He says saving faith "is reliance on the truth of the gospel as revealed in the Word of God" (Ryrie, *BT*, p. 327).

Gordon Clark Pointing out that in Matthew 18:6 and Mark 9:42, Jesus said that children believe in (*eis*) Me, even Clark, who strongly believes that faith is belief in a proposition, says, "If anyone wishes to say that children *trusted* in him, well and good;

to trust is to believe *that* good will follow" (Clark, p. 99).

Zane Hodges Originally, Zane Hodges was willing to use the word trust. He wrote, "Thus, by believing the amazing facts about the person of Christ, Martha was trusting Him. She was placing her eternal destiny in His hands" (Hodges, *AF*, 1989, p. 39).

If faith is trust, what is the content of the trust? It is trusting Jesus Christ, who died to pay for sin and rose from the dead, *for* the gift of eternal life (1 Tim. 1:16 NKJV), *for* the forgiveness of sins (Acts 10:43), *for* salvation (Acts 16:31), or to get me to heaven (Jn. 14:1-6). "To trust Christ [is] … to rest upon Him for salvation" (Machen, p. 13).

Faith is Mental, Emotional, and Volitional

Some Christians teach that faith involves the emotions, and/or the will, and/or both, as well as mental assent.

The Emotions Many preachers proclaim that faith involves feelings. They say that some people believe the gospel with their heads but not with their hearts, implying that if no heartfelt emotion is present, neither is faith.

The Will For some, faith involves the will. In the Roman Catholic *Dogmatic Decrees of the Vatican* Council (1870), the chapter on faith says, "We are bound to yield to God, by faith in his revelation, the full obedience of our intelligence and will…. The act of faith is a work pertaining to salvation, by which man yields volunteer obedience to God himself, by asserting to and cooperating with his grace, which he is able to resist" (*Dogmatic*

Decrees, cited by Clark, pp. 38-39).

All Three Some theologians contend that faith involves the mind, emotions, and will. For example, Berkhof says there are intellectual, emotional, and volitional elements in faith (Berkhof, pp. 503-506). As for the emotional element, he says, "It is so difficult to make a clear distinction; some theologians prefer to speak of only two elements in saving faith, namely, knowledge and personal trust" (Berkhof, p. 505). In other words, he acknowledges that faith has an emotional element, but finds it very difficult to demonstrate, and ultimately denies it.

Faith is Commitment

Rudolph Bultmann Rudolph Bultmann states, faith "is a man's absolute committal to God, a committal in which man cannot make any resolutions of his own.... It is indeed the radical decision of the will in which a man delivers himself up" (Bultmann in Kittel, vol. 6, p. 219). He says, "To believe is to obey" (Bultmann in Kittel, *Theological Dictionary of New Testament*, vol. 6, p. 205).

John R. Stott John R. Stott says, "Faith is directed towards a Person. It is, in fact, a complete commitment to this Person involving not only an acceptance of what is offered but a humble surrender to what is or may be demanded. The bent knee is as much a part of saving faith as the open hand. It is impossible to come to Christ with words like "Nothing in my hand I bring" and at the same time deliberately to withhold one's personal allegiance. Our Jesus Christ fulfills many roles, but He is one person, and faith is a commitment to Him as a whole person, not in a particular role. Faith may not choose to be committed to Him in the role of Savior and not in the role of the Lord" (Stott, p. 17).

Paul Little Paul Little puts it this way: "It involves total commitment of intellect, emotions, and will. One must believe in Jesus Christ and personally receive Him into one's life; and thus become a child of God" (Little, p. 59).

John MacArthur John MacArthur wrote, "The faith God begets includes both the volition and the ability to comply with His will (compare Philippians 2:13). In other words, faith encompasses obedience" (MacArthur, p. 173). MacArthur concludes, "Clearly, the biblical concept of faith is inseparable from obedience" (MacArthur, p. 174). He then quotes Berkhof, who, he says, sees three elements in genuine faith—an intellectual element, which is the understanding of the truth, an emotional element, which is the conviction and affirmation of the truth "and a volitional element (*Fiducia*) which is the determination of the will to obey truth" (MacArthur, p. 173, who cites Berkhof, p. 505).

On page 505, Berkhof does not say that the volitional element is "the determination of the will to obey the truth." He says, "it [faith] is also a matter of the will, determining the direction of the soul, an act of the soul going out toward its object and appropriating this…. This third element [volition] consists of a personal trust in Christ as Savior and Lord, including a surrender of the soul, which is guilty and defiled to Christ, and a reception and appropriation of Christ, which is the source of pardon and of spiritual life" (Berkhof, p. 505). Nowhere on page 505 does

Berkhof say that the volitional element in faith is the determination of the will to obey the truth.

Ryrie observed the same thing. He says, "Berkhof does not inject or speak of the issue of the mastery of Christ over one's life when discussing these three elements of faith. His third aspect, *fiducia* [the Latin word for faith], concerns the involvement of the human will and personal trust in the Lord for salvation, not commitment of the years of one's life to his mastery (contrary to MacArthur)" (Ryrie, *So Great Salvation*, p. 120).

Hodges says that MacArthur "seriously distorts" Berkhof's definition of faith, adding it is "astonishingly inaccurate" (Hodges, *LS*, p. 207).

Summary: Various views of saving faith among Christians include: faith is mental assent to a proposition, belief in a promise, trust in Jesus, faith includes intellect, emotion, and will, and commitment.

Chapter 2

The Bible Explanation of Faith

As we have seen (see Introduction), the Bible teaches that salvation is by faith alone in Christ alone. Salvation is by faith in the Old Testament as well as in the New Testament. In the Old Testament, this concept is taught in Genesis 15:6 and Habakkuk 2:4. In the Gospel of John, it is stated that when people believe, they have *eternal life* (Jn. 3:36; etc.). In Romans and Galatians, *justification* is by faith (Rom. 3:26, 28, 30; 4:3, 5, 9, 11, 13, 16, 20-22, 24; 5:1; Gal. 3:6, 8, 11, 24). In Acts, the issue is the *forgiveness* of sins (Acts 2:38; 5:11; 10:43; 13:38; 26:38; Jesus commissioned them to preach the remission of sins, Lk. 24:47). In addition, people are said to be the *children of God* by faith (Jn. 1:12; Gal. 3:26). What is the biblical definition and content of saving faith?

The Definition of Faith

The Hebrew Words Genesis 15:6 says, "And he [Abraham] believed in the LORD, and He accounted it to him for righteousness." The Hebrew word translated "believed" means "to confirm, to be established, make firm, to trust, to be certain, to believe in" (BDB, Hebrew lexicon). English translations of Genesis 15:6 render it "believed" (KJV; NKJV; NASB; NIV; ESV).

Also, in this verse, "believed" is in the perfect tense (the perfect tense describes past action with present results). In other words, Abram did not come to faith here (Ross; Leupold; Constable). At some point in the past, he had believed in the Lord, which led to his continued belief in the present.

The construction of the Hebrew word "believe" in Genesis 15:6 (believe plus the proposition "in") "refers to "a confident resting on a person or thing or testimony" (Berkhof, p. 493). The ancient Greek translation of the Old Testament (the Septuagint) uses the same Greek word for "believe" and "in" is the same construction ["believe" followed by the preposition "in" (*eis*)] that is used in the Gospel of John (Jn. 3:16; etc.). B. B. Warfield, the famous 19th-century Princeton professor and a great defender of inerrancy, says, "To believe in God, in the Old Testament sense, is thus not merely to assent to His word, but ... to rest ... upon Him" (Warfield, in *Biblical Doctrine*, 1929, p. 471).

Prior to Genesis 15, the Lord had promised Abram that in him "all the families of the earth shall be blessed" (Gen. 12:3), a promise that included the coming of the Messiah, who would be a descendant of Abram. Jesus said, "Abraham rejoiced to see My day, and he saw *it* and was glad" (Jn. 8:56), a reference to Genesis 12:3 (Blum, on John 8:56 in the *Bible Knowledge Commentary*). In other words, sometime before Genesis 15, Abram *trusted* the *Lord* ("believed in") and the Lord counted it to him for righteousness. Abram trusted a *person* and, as a result, was declared righteous. Abram then began to live by faith. Abram trusted the Lord (Gen. 15:6) to fulfill the *promise* of the Messiah. He left Ur by faith (Heb. 11:8) and was trusting the Lord in Genesis 15.

The Lord had promised Abram a son (Gen. 12:2, 7; 13:14-17). In Genesis 15, Abram reminds the Lord that he was childless (Gen. 15:2-3). The Lord responded that He would give him a son and as many descendants as there are stars in heaven (Gen. 15:4-5). In that context, the reader is reminded that Abram had believed in the Lord in the past (Gen. 15:6) and believed in the Lord in the present (the meaning of the perfect tense). That comment is inserted here to indicate that although Abram pointedly asked God about His promise concerning a son (Gen. 15:2-3), he believed the *promise* the Lord just gave him. Note that Abram trusted a *person* to fulfill a *promise*.

To prove that salvation is by faith, Paul quotes Genesis 15:6 (Rom. 4:3, see also Gal. 3:6; Heb. 10:38). In Romans 4, Paul says, "Therefore *it is* of faith that *it might be* according to grace, so that the *promise* might be sure to all the seed, not only to those who are of the law, but also to those who are of the faith of Abraham, who is the father of us all (as it is written, 'I have made you a father of many nations') in the presence of Him whom he believed—God, who gives life to the dead and calls those things which do not exist as though they did; who, contrary to hope, in hope believed, so that he became the father of many nations, according to what was spoken, 'so shall your descendants be.' And not being weak in faith, he did not consider his own body, already dead (since he was about a hundred years old), and the deadness of Sarah's womb. He did not waver at the *promise* of God through unbelief, but was strengthened in faith, giving glory to God and being *fully convinced* that what He had *promised* He was also able to perform. And therefore, 'It was accounted to him for righteousness'" (Rom. 4:16-22; italics added).

Abram believed in the Lord (Gen. 15:6); he was *fully convinced* that what God *promised* to do, He was able to do (Rom. 4:21), including giving life to a dead womb (Rom. 4:17, 19). That is the kind of faith that saved Abram. Abram "believed in the Lord." He trusted the Lord to fulfill His promise.

Conclusion: Genesis 15:6 teaches that justification (being declared righteous) is by trusting the Lord, believing what He promised is true, and being confident He will fulfill His promise. From this, it can be concluded that believing *in* a person means trusting that individual *for* something. In Abram's case, he "believed in the Lord" for salvation, and he believed in the Lord to fulfill His promise to give him a son.

Habakkuk 2:4 says, "Behold the proud, His soul is not upright in him, but the just shall live by his faith." Technically, the Old Testament does not contain a noun for "faith" unless Habakkuk 2:4 is considered (Berkhof, p. 493). The Hebrew word translated "faith" in Habakkuk 2:4 means "firmness, fidelity, steadfastness, steadiness" (BDB Hebrew lexicon). Paul quotes Habakkuk 2:4 in Galatians 3:11 to demonstrate that justification is by faith.

In the context of Habakkuk 2, Habakkuk 2:4 is saying an *already justified* person should live by faith, that is, trust the Lord to judge righteously. If Habakkuk 2:4 talks about a person who is *already justified,* how can Paul use it to prove that *sinners* are justified by faith? One answer is if the justified are to live by faith, the *inference* is that life is the result of faith (Eadie on Gal. 3:11). Another answer is that Paul is not interpreting the verse; he is applying the verse (Fung on Gal. 3:11). Cole says, "Paul does not prove his doctrine of 'justification by faith' from this verse; he only illustrates it. He proves it from God's way of dealing with Abraham. This verse is nothing more than a handy peg upon which to hang a spiritual truth abundantly clear elsewhere in Scripture" (Cole on Gal. 3:11).

Conclusion: According to Habakkuk 2:4, a righteous man before God should live by faith, which means trusting God to do what is right. That implies that since people are to live by faith, they were declared righteous by faith.

The Greek Words The Arndt and Gingrich lexicon says the Greek verb translated "believe" means "believe (in) something; be convinced of something." The Moulton and Milligan Greek lexicon translates the Greek word for "believe" as "trust" (Moulton and Milligan, p. 514). The Liddell and Scott Greek-English lexicon says "believe" means "to trust, trust to," or "in," "put faith in, rely on, believe" a person or thing (Liddell and Scott,

p. 641). A statement in Kittel says, "From a purely formal standpoint, there is nothing very distinctive" in the usage of the New Testament writings as compared with usage in secular Greek usage. As in secular Greek, it means "to rely on," "to trust," "to believe" (Kittel, vol. VI, p. 203). Likewise, the Greek noun translated "faith" means "trust, confidence" (Arndt and Gingrich lexicon).

When "believe" is used with the preposition in (Greek: *eis*), the Arndt and Gingrich lexicon says it means "depend on, put one's trust in and that it can also mean to entrust something to someone. The Abbott-Smith Greek lexicon says that when the verb "believe" is followed by the preposition "in" (Greek: *eis*), it is "expressing personal trust and reliance as distinct from credence or belief."

Conclusion: The Greek words translated "believe" and "faith" mean to accept something as true and trust it. When the preposition "in" (Greek: *eis*) is added to the verb "believe," it emphasizes the aspect of trust.

The Content of Faith

Saving faith involves knowledge. People cannot believe something they do not know. What knowledge is necessary for saving faith?

The Gospel of John Part of the purpose of the Gospel of John is to tell people how to have eternal life, that is, how to be saved (being "saved" is used for being given spiritual life in Eph. 2:4, where "made us alive" is explained as "you have been saved"). At the end of his book, John states, "And truly Jesus did many other signs in the presence of His disciples, which are not written in this book. But these are written that you may believe that Jesus is the Christ, the Son of God, and that believing you may have life in His name" (Jn. 20:30-31). The signs/miracles in the Gospel of John are written to convince the reader of two things: 1) Jesus is the Christ, that is, the Messiah, and 2) Jesus is the Son of God, that is, God in the flesh.

When John wrote his book, he did not chop it up into chapters and verses; that was done later. He did not intend for people to take a few statements out of the book to draw a conclusion. He meant for people to read the *whole book*. If they did that, they would conclude that Jesus, the Messiah, God in the flesh, died for the sins of the world and rose from the dead, and if they believed *in* Him (trusted Him *for* eternal life), they would have everlasting life.

The Gospel of John begins by declaring that Jesus is God (Jn. 1:1), that Jesus is the Lamb of God who takes away the sin of the world (Jn. 1:29), that Jesus must die (Jn. 3:14), and that Jesus is the Messiah (Jn. 1:41; 4:25-26). That is only the beginning of the book! Taken as a whole, it is inescapable that John is saying Jesus is the Messiah, the Son of God, who died and rose from the dead.

What does being the Messiah mean? The Gospel of John does not explicitly explain what about Jesus being the Messiah is necessary to believe to have eternal life, but Jesus explains it, and Luke records what He said. Luke records, "He [Jesus] opened their understanding that they might comprehend the Scriptures.

Then He said to them, 'Thus it is written, and thus it was necessary for the Christ [the Greek word for Messiah] to suffer and to rise from the dead the third day'" (Lk. 24:45-46).

Concerning Paul's ministry, Luke says, "Then Paul, as his custom was, went in to them, and for three Sabbath reasoned with them from the Scripture, explaining and demonstrating that Christ had to suffer and rise again from the dead, and *saying*, 'This Jesus whom I preached to you is the Christ'" (Acts 17:2-3).

Luke left no doubt that Jesus and Paul believed that the definition of being "the Christ" was that the Messiah would die and be raised from the dead.

The construction "believe that" occurs twelve times in John's Gospel. The "believe that" construction delineates facts to be believed. These facts are that Jesus is the Christ, the Son of God (11:27; 20:31), who is God (8:24; 10:38; 13:19; 14:10; 14:11), sent by the Father (11:42; 16:27, 16:30; 17:8, 17:21). The construction "believe in" occurs thirty-seven times in the Gospel of John. As has been pointed out, "believe in" emphasizes trust. It is a unique construction. Dodd does not find "believe in" in secular Greek (Dodd, p. 183, cited by Morris, p. 335, fn. 131). Does not the fact that John uses a unique construction so many times imply there is a difference between "believe that" and "believe in"? Also, is it not significant that Greek lexicons conclude such things as: when used in the religious sense, "believe (in)," has a "special emphasis on trust" (Arndt and Gingrich 2nd, p. 661) and "believe in" means, "personal trust and reliance as distinct from mere credence or belief" (Abbott-Smith, pp. 361-362).

In addition, the Gospel of John uses synonyms for "believe." Figures for faith include asking (Jn. 4:10), drinking water (Jn. 4:13-14), doing the good thing (Jn. 5:29), and working (Jn. 6:20-29). Jesus tells people to labor for eternal life (Jn. 6:27) but clarifies that the Son of Man *gives* eternal life, indicating it is a gift (Jn. 6:27). He says, "I am the bread of life. He who comes to Me shall never hunger, and he who believes in Me shall never thirst" (Jn. 6:35). Coming to Christ and believing in Him are synonymous in this statement, as are "never hungering and never thirsting" (Jn. 6:53). He says, "This is the bread which comes down from heaven, that one may eat of it and not die. I am the living bread that came down from heaven. If anyone eats of this bread, he will live forever; and the bread that I shall give is My flesh, which I shall give for the life of the world" (Jn. 6:50-51). He says, "Whoever eats My flesh and drinks My blood has eternal life, and I will raise him up at the last day" (Jn. 6:54). Jesus uses the figure of walking as a synonym for faith (Jn. 12:35), which is clear from the next verse (Jn. 12:36; see also Jn. 5:11). He even uses "following" as a synonym for faith (Jn. 10:27).

Asking, drinking, doing, working, laboring, coming, eating, walking, and following are figures of speech for believing, indicating that believing is more than believing a proportion. These metaphors convey the concept of appropriation by trusting or depending on something or someone. For example, eating bread indicates dependence on bread for life. On the other hand, these metaphors should not be taken to teach that anyone can do anything meritorious; eternal life is not by works. It is a gift (Jn.

4:10). Therefore, saving faith involves *both* "believing that" and "believing in" (Bruce, *John,* p. 12). The difference is that "believe that" is being convinced that something is true, and "believe in" conveys the concept of trust, reliance on, or dependence on someone (Jesus) for something (eternal life). As Erickson says, "The type of faith necessary for salvation involves believing that and believing in or assenting to facts and trusting in a person" (Erickson, p. 940).

It is obvious there is a difference between believing facts and trusting those facts. I can believe the plane will get me someplace without trusting it to do it. John desires his readers to believe that Jesus is the Christ, the Son of God, who died for the sins of the world and rose from the dead; he wants them to *trust Jesus for eternal life.*

Conclusion: According to the Gospel of John, the content of believing in Jesus for eternal life is believing that Jesus is the Christ, the Son of God, who died and rose from the dead. Some challenge that conclusion, pointing out that the disciples did not believe in the resurrection until after the resurrection (Jn. 20:9). That is true, but from the beginning, they believed that Jesus was the Messiah (Jn. 1:41). They didn't understand that the Messiah was going to be raised from the dead. In other words, *before the resurrection,* people were saved by believing in the Messiah, even if they didn't fully understand everything involved. The Gospel of John was written after the resurrection to explain that Jesus is the Christ, the Son of God, who died and was raised from the dead. So, *after the resurrection,* people had to believe more than those who lived before it. They had to believe in Jesus (Jn. 14:6; Acts 4:12), the Christ, the One who came to die for the sins of the world and be raised from the dead.

The Formula: There seems to be a "formula" for believing in the New Testament. The definition of the English word "formula" is "a set form of words, as for stating or declaring something definitive authoritatively."

Jesus asked the disciples, "But who do you say that I am?" (Mt. 16:15). In the Greek text, the word "you" is emphatic. The issue is not what others think. It is what *you* believe. "Simon Peter answered and said, 'You are the Christ, the Son of the living God'" (Mt. 16:16; see also Jn. 6:69: "We have come to believe and know that You are the Christ, the Son of the living God"). The disciples believed that Jesus is the Messiah, the Son of God.

Later, Jesus said to Martha, "I am the resurrection and the life. He who believes in Me, though he may die, he shall live. And whoever lives and believes in Me shall never die. Do you believe this?" (Jn. 11:25-26). Jesus says two things about Himself. First, He says He is the resurrection and some, like Lazarus, believe in (*eis*) Him and die; they shall live. Morris says the Greek construction signifies "personal trust." Second, Jesus says that He is the life and some, like Martha, who are still living, believe in (*eis*) Him; they shall never die. In other words, if they trust Christ for eternal life, they will never die because they will live eternally.

Then, Jesus pointedly asked Martha, "Do you believe this (*oti*)?" In other words, Jesus asked Martha if she believed that (*oti*) trusting in Him (*eis*) meant that she would have eternal life. "She said to Him, 'Yes, Lord, I believe that You are the Christ, the Son of God, who is come into the world'" (Jn. 11:27). In the Greek text, the word "I" is emphatic. Martha emphatically declares that she believes Jesus is the Messiah, the Son of God. For John, this is a climax in his Gospel. As he states at the end of his book, he wrote that people may believe that Jesus is the Christ, the Son of God (Jn. 20:31). Martha makes that very confession.

Still later, Philip said to the Ethiopian, "If you believe with all your heart, you may and he answered and said, 'I believe that Jesus Christ is the Son of God'" (Acts 8:37). This verse is not in the Critical Greek Text, nor is it in the Majority Text. It is, however, in the *Textus Receptus* (the traditional Greek text). Pointing out that Cyprian and Irenaeus quote it, Alexander concludes that the scale is tipped in favor of the *Received Text*. At any rate, notice that the confession is virtually the same as the one the disciples and Martha gave.

John wrote, "And truly Jesus did many other signs in the presence of His disciples, which are not written in this book; but these are written that you may believe that Jesus is the Christ, the Son of God and that believing you may have life in His name" (Jn. 20:30-31).

This "formula," Jesus is the Christ, the Son of God, seems to be the definitive statement in the New Testament of what people must believe to be saved. It is the only statement repeated several times, and it is part of the purpose of the Gospel of John. People must believe that Jesus is the Christ (Greek for Messiah), which He says means believing He died and rose (Lk. 24:45-46) and that

He is the Son of God to have eternal life.

The Objects of Faith "If you were to look up all the occurrences of 'believe' and 'faith' in the New Testament to see what a person must know about Christ, you would discover four things: (1) that Christ is God (Jn. 20:31) and yet (2) a real man (1 Jn. 4:2), (3) that He is the one who died for sins (Rom. 3:25), and (4) rose from the dead (Rom. 10:9)" (G. Michael Cocoris, *Evangelism A Biblical Approach*, revised edition, 2018, pp. 68-69; this also appears in the original 1984 edition).

The Gospel Whatever people believed to be saved before the death and resurrection of Jesus Christ, it is abundantly clear that after the death and resurrection of Christ, we are to preach the gospel. The only passage in the New Testament that defines the gospel is in 1 Corinthians 15, which says the gospel is that Christ died for our sins and rose from the dead (1 Cor. 15:3-5).

In the **Great Commission**, Jesus commands the apostles to evangelize by preaching the gospel. Jesus said, "Go into all the world and preach the gospel to every creature" (Mk. 16:15).

In Acts, **Peter** evangelized by preaching the gospel (Acts 15:7). For example, in Acts 13:32, he said that he was declaring "glad tidings" (Greek: the gospel) to the people at the synagogue in Antioch Pisidia. He preached the humanity (Acts 13:23), the deity (Acts 13:34), death (Acts 13:28; see "the tree" in verse 29), and resurrection (Acts 13:30, 33-37) of Jesus Christ.

Paul did the same thing. "Then Paul, as his custom was, went in to them, and for three Sabbaths reasoned with them from the Scriptures, explaining and demonstrating that the Christ had to suffer and rise again from the dead, and *saying,* 'This Jesus whom I preach to you is the Christ'" (Acts 17:2-3). Note: "**as his custom was.**" "They [Paul and Barnabas] were preaching the gospel there [see Lystra and Derbe, cities of Lycaonia, and to the surrounding region in Acts 14:7]" (Acts 14:6). But some had "questions against him about their own religion and about a certain Jesus, who had died, whom Paul affirmed to be alive" (Acts 25:19).

"Therefore, having obtained help from God, to this day I stand, witnessing both to small and great, saying no other things than those which the prophets and Moses said would come—that the Christ would suffer, that He would be the first to rise from the dead, and would proclaim light to the *Jewish* people and to the Gentiles" (Acts 26:22-23). "I [Paul] have made it my aim to preach the gospel, not where Christ was named, lest I should build on another man's foundation" (Rom. 15:20).

When Paul evangelized the **Corinthians**, he preached the gospel. "Moreover, brethren, I declare to you the gospel which I preached to you, which also you received and in which you stand, by which also you are saved, if you hold fast that word which I preached to you—unless you believed in vain. For I delivered to you first of all that which I also received: that Christ died for our sins according to the Scriptures, and that He was buried, and that He rose again the third day according to the Scriptures" (1 Cor. 15:1-4).

When Paul evangelized the **Galatians**, he preached the gospel. "O foolish Galatians! Who has bewitched you that you should not obey the truth, before whose eyes Jesus Christ was clearly portrayed among you as crucified?" (Gal. 3:1).

When Paul evangelized the **Ephesians**, he preached the gospel. "In Him you also *trusted,* after you heard the word of truth, the gospel of your salvation; in whom also, having believed, you were sealed with the Holy Spirit of promise" (Eph. 1:13).

When Paul evangelized the **Praetorian Guard** in Rome, he preached the Gospel. "I want you to know, brethren, that the things *which happened* to me have actually turned out for the furtherance of the gospel" (Phil. 1:12).

When Paul evangelized the **Philippians**, he preached the gospel. "Now you Philippians know also that in the beginning of the gospel, when I departed from Macedonia, no church shared with me concerning giving and receiving but you only" (Phil. 4:15).

When Paul evangelized the **Colossians**, he preached the gospel "because of the hope which is laid up for you in heaven, of which you heard before in the word of the truth of the gospel" (Col 1:5).

When Paul evangelized the **Thessalonians**, he preached the gospel. "For our gospel did not come to you in word only, but also in power, and in the Holy Spirit and in much assurance, as you know what kind of men we were among you for your sake" (1 Thess. 1:5). For you remember, brethren, our labor and toil; for laboring night and day, that we might not be a burden to any of you, we preached to you the gospel of God" (1 Thes. 2:9). "He called you by our gospel, for the obtaining of the glory of our Lord Jesus Christ" (2 Thess. 2:14).

Philip, the only evangelist in the New Testament, preached about Jesus based on Isaiah 53, which includes the death and resurrection of Christ. "Then Philip opened his mouth, and beginning at this Scripture [Isa. 53], preached Jesus to him" (Acts 8:35).

James and others were saved through the gospel. "Of His own will, He brought us forth by the word of truth" (Jas. 1:18, where "word of truth" is another name for the gospel; see Eph. 1:13).

In other words, according to the command of Jesus, the examples of Peter, Paul, and Philip, and the epistles of Paul and James, to evangelize, we are to preach the gospel.

The Promise The New Testament speaks of believing the promise of God to be saved. Paul says, "He [Abraham] did not waver at the promise of God through unbelief, but was strengthened in faith, giving glory to God, and being fully convinced that what He had promised He was also able to perform. And therefore, 'It was accounted to him for righteousness'" (Rom. 4:20-22). Paul's point is that when Abraham believed God's promise to him, his faith was counted as righteousness. Then Paul applies that to people living today. He says, "Now it was not written for his sake alone that it was imputed to him, but also for us. It shall be imputed to us who believe in Him who raised up Jesus our Lord from the dead, who was delivered up because of our offenses, and was raised because of our justification" (Rom. 4:23-25). Like Abraham, people are declared righteous when they believe God's promise to declare us righteous, based on Jesus being delivered up for our offenses and being raised from the dead.

John was concerned that antichrists were trying to deceive believers. So he wrote, "Who is a liar but he who denies that Jesus is the Christ? He is an antichrist who denies the Father and the Son. Whoever denies the Son does not have the Father either; he who acknowledges the Son has the Father also. Therefore, let that abide in you which you heard from the beginning. If what you heard from the beginning abides in you, you also will abide in the Son and in the Father. And this is the promise that He has promised us—eternal life" (1 Jn. 2:22-25). The antichrists were trying to deceive believers concerning Jesus being the Messiah, the Son of God, who gave the promise of eternal life.

The Nature of Faith

The philosophical question, and, for some, the theological question, is, "Is faith active or passive? Some philosophers and theologians argue that faith is passive, suggesting that people do not choose to believe; instead, they see the truth and accept it passively. They walk into a room with a light on, and they believe it is on. They do not choose to believe; they just see and believe. There is truth in that, but the New Testament does not hesitate to speak of faith as being active. Jesus speaks of people choosing to come to Him or not. He says, "On the last day, that great *day* of the feast, Jesus stood and cried out, saying, 'If anyone thirsts, let him come to Me and drink. He who believes in Me, as the Scripture has said, out of his heart will flow rivers of living water'" (Jn. 7:37-38: see also 6:44, 65) and "You are not willing to come to

Me that you may have life" (Jn. 5:40; see also Mt, 23:37). Figurative expressions for faith indicated that faith is active, include looking [Jn. 3:14, 15 (see Num. 21:9), drinking (Jn. 4:14), eating (Jn. 6:50-58), etc.].

Summary: The faith required to get to heaven is trust in Jesus Christ *for* the gift of eternal life [1 Tim. 1:16 NKJV, or *for* the forgiveness of sins (Acts 10:43), or *for* salvation (Acts 16:31), or to get me to heaven (Jn. 14:1-6)]. And the content of that faith is the gospel, namely that Jesus Christ died for sin and rose from the dead, which is demonstrated by 1) the Gospel of John, 2) the objects of faith throughout the New Testament, 3) the command of the Great Commission, and 4) the practice of Peter, Paul, Philip, and James.

What about Hebrews 11:1? Hebrews 11 begins with several statements about faith (Heb. 11:1-3). The first is, "Now faith is the substance of things hoped for, the evidence of things not seen" (Heb. 11:1). Many say that this opening statement is not a definition of faith (Westcott; Guthrie); it is a description of what faith does (Kent). The Greek word translated "substance" means "substantial nature, essence, reality" (see "person" in Heb. 1:3). That meaning was uniformly adopted by ancient commentators (Westcott). Modern commentators, however, have accepted a subjective sense of "confidence" (Alford; Bruce; Kent). Scholars have recently decided that this word means "realization" (A-G). The future is made real for men of faith, that is, things "hoped for" in the future truly exist and this existence of faith brings home to the believer as fact (Westcott).

Faith is the evidence of things not seen. The Greek word rendered "evidence" means "proof, test" (A-S). Faith is the proof by which the unseen is established (Westcott). Faith enables us to treat as real unseen things (Dods, *Expos. Gk. NT*). Faith makes the unseen real to me. In the context of Hebrews, these future ("hoped for") unseen things include the believer's future blessings at the return of Christ (10:35-37; Kent). Faith treats those future things as realities.

"Now faith is the assurance of things hoped for, a conviction of things not seen" (ASV; *The Darby Translation* also uses the word "conviction"). "Now faith is the assurance of *things* hoped for, the conviction of things not seen" (NASB). "Now faith is being sure of what we hope for and certain of what we do not see" (NIV).

Faith is the assurance of conviction. It is being persuaded. John Calvin calls faith a "full persuasion" of truth (Calvin, *Institutes*, III. ii. 12). Imagine being on a jury and saying, "I believe the defendant is guilty. I am persuaded he committed the crime." In other words, "believe" and "persuaded" are synonyms.

Faith sees the invisible, but it does not see the nonexistent. Faith believes facts, not fables. Before Orville and Wilbur Wright made their first flight, mathematicians and scientists had proven that flight was possible. Nevertheless, even though they knew the facts, many did not believe flying would ever become a reality. The Wright brothers believed the facts. Their faith enabled them to see the reality. On December 17, 1903, they experienced the reality.

In short, *Faith is confident that the unseen future is real.*

Chapter 3

The Conversion of Famous Christians

In light of what the Bible, various Christians, and theologians have said about faith, it is interesting to review some famous conversions in church history to see how they measure up to the biblical explanation of faith.

Augustine

In 385, Augustine was converted. In his *Confessions*, he describes his conversion. "I probed the hidden depths of my soul and wrung its pitiful secrets from it, and when I gathered them all before the eyes of my heart, a great storm broke within me, bringing with it a great deluge of tears … For I felt that I was still enslaved by my sins, and in my misery, I kept crying, 'How long shall I go on saying tomorrow, tomorrow? Why not now? Why not make an end of my ugly sins at this moment?'

"I was asking myself these questions, weeping all the while with the most bitter sorrow in my heart, when all at once I heard the sing-song voice of a child in a nearby house. Whether it was the voice of a boy or girl, I cannot say, but again and again, it repeated the chorus, 'Take it and read, take it and read.' At this, I looked up, thinking hard whether there was any kind of game in which children used to chant words like these, but I could not remember ever hearing them before. I stemmed my flood of tears and stood up, telling myself that this could only be God's command to open my book of Scripture and read the first passage on which my eyes should fall. For I had heard the story of Antony, and I remembered how he had happened to go into a church while the Gospel was being read and had taken it as an instruction addressed to himself when he heard the words, 'Go home and sell all that belongs to you. Give it to the poor, and so the treasure you have shall be in heaven; then come back and follow me.' By this message from God, he had at once been converted.

"So I hurried back to the place where Alypius was sitting, for when I stood up to move away, I had put down the book containing Paul's Letters. I seized it and opened it, and in silence, I read the first passage on which my eyes fell: 'No orgies or drunkenness, no immorality or indecency, no fighting or jealousy. Take up the weapons of the Lord Jesus Christ, and stop giving attention to your sinful nature to satisfy its desires.' I had no wish to read more and no need to do so. For in an instant, as I came to the end of the sentence, it was as though the light of faith flooded into my heart and the darkness of doubt was dispelled" (Augustine, *Confessions* 12).

Martin Luther

When he was struggling spiritually, Martin Luther cried out to Johann von Staupitz, the head of the Augustinian order in Germany, "Oh, my sins! My sins! My sins!" Staupitz replied, "Remember that Christ came into the world for the pardon of our sins." On another occasion, when the thought of Christ terrified Luther because he thought of the Lord as the One who punishes sin, Staupitz told him, "Your thoughts are not according to Christ; Christ does not terrify, he consoles. Look at the wounds of Christ and you will there see shining clearly the purpose of God towards men" (Houghton, p. 81). Staupitz urged Luther to trust God and study the Bible (Cairns, p. 289).

In 1510, when Luther went to Rome, he climbed Pilate's stairs on his bare knees. In one of his sermons, he refers to that experience. He said, "I wish to liberate my grandfather from purgatory and went up the staircase of Pilate, praying a *pater noster* (Latin: 'our Father,' a reference to the Lord's Prayer) on each step; for I was convinced that he who prayed thus could redeem his soul. But when I came to the top step, I thought, 'Who knows whether this is true?'" An account written by his youngest son, Paul, says that as his father ascended the staircase, the words of Habakkuk came to his mind, "The just shall live by faith," which caused him to realize the worthlessness of stair-climbing (Houghton, pp. 83-84).

Scholars differ concerning the date of Luther's conversion. Some say it occurred at the end of 1512 when, in his room in the tower of the Black Cloister, he read, "The just shall live by faith" in Romans 1:17 (Kuiper, p. 163). Others claim his understanding of the doctrine of justification by faith probably came in 1515 when he began teaching the book of Romans. After struggling with Romans 1:17, which says, "The righteousness of God is revealed from faith to faith; as it is written, 'the just shall live by faith,'" Luther realized the righteousness of God is given to those who live by faith. "The righteousness or justice of God is not the justice by which God punishes sin but the justice by which he makes us just" (Cary, *Luther*, vol. 1, p. 16). Concerning this discovery, Luther said, "I felt that I had been born anew and that the gates of heaven had been opened, the whole of Scripture gained a new meaning" (González, II, pp. 19-20). Luther found peace for his soul, which he had not been able to find in rites, acts of asceticism, or the mystics' theology (Cairns, p. 289).

John Calvin

Little is known of Calvin's conversion. It has been dated between 1527 and 1534. Parker argues for a date between late 1529 and early 1530 (Parker, pp. 162-165). Calvin's only reference to his conversion is recorded in his preface to his commentary on the Psalms. He compares himself to David, saying that as David was taken from the sheepfold and raised on the throne, so he had been raised from obscure origins and made a minister of the gospel (Parker, p. 22).

Calvin wrote, "My father had intended me for theology from my early childhood…. Then, changing his mind, he set me to learning law ... until God, at last, turned my course in another direction by the secret rein of his providence. By a sudden conversion, he turned to teachableness a mind too stubborn for its years, for I was so strongly devoted to the superstitions of the papacy that nothing less could draw me from such depths of mire" (Calvin, cited by Houghton, p. 103, who explains "a sudden conversion" as "unexpected").

John Wesley

In 1735, John and Charles Wesley sailed to Georgia, America, to become missionaries. During the voyage, the ship encountered a storm that was so severe that its mainmast split. The Moravians on board were unbelievably calm, even singing throughout the ordeal. They told John Wesley they had behaved so bravely because they did not fear death, a comment that led Wesley to begin to doubt the depth of his own faith (González, II, p. 209).

August Spangenberg, the leader of the Moravian settlement in Georgia, asked John if he knew Jesus Christ. When John told him that he knew Jesus was the Savior of the world, Spangenberg asked, "Do you know that He has saved you?" For the next three years, that question preyed on John's mind because he was not sure of the answer (Kuiper, p. 286). John later said, "I who went to America to convert others was never converted to God myself." He also said, "I diligently strove against sin, I omitted no sort of self-denial which I thought lawful. I omitted no occasion of doing good, but could not find that all this gave me any assurance of acceptance with God." Concerning the witness of the Moravians, he said, "I understood it not at first. I was to learn to be wise so that it seemed foolishness to me. I continued preaching, and following after, and trusting in that righteousness wherein no flesh can be justified" (Houghton, pp. 188-189).

John and Charles labored with all their might in Georgia. John was a linguist; he knew many languages well. He preached in English, German, French, and Italian. Despite all their efforts, John and Charles were unsuccessful in their mission to Georgia. A year after their arrival, Charles fell ill and returned to England (Kuiper, p. 287). Because of his strictness and frankness, John was forced to go home in 1737 (Cairns, p. 383).

Back in England, John and Charles became acquainted with Peter Bohler, a Moravian, who taught "a faith of complete self-surrender, instantaneous conversion, and joy in believing" (Kuiper, p. 287). In his *Journal,* Wesley writes that Peter Bohler convinced him that salvation was by faith alone, but since he didn't yet have it, he considered ceasing to preach. Bohler told him, "Preach faith until you have it; and then, because you have it." That is what Wesley did. He preached salvation by faith alone before he trusted Christ (Wesley's *Journal,* March 4, 1738, p. 58; see also the journal entry on April 25, 1738, p. 61 and May 14, 1738, p. 63). Charles was converted on May 21, 1738 (Kuiper, p. 287).

On May 24, 1738, John attended a Moravian meetinghouse in London (Houghton, p. 189) on Aldersgate Street (Mead, p. 218), where, while listening to the reading of Luther's preface to his

Commentary on Romans, he was converted (Cairns, p. 383). He was 34 years old at the time (Kuiper, p. 287). He described what happened: "About a quarter before nine, while I was listening to Luther's description of the change which God works in the heart through faith in Christ, I felt my heart strangely warmed. I felt I did trust Christ, Christ alone, for salvation; and an assurance was given to me, that He had taken away my sins, even mine, and saved me from the law of sin and death" (Wesley's *Journal*, March 24, 1738, p. 64). John's experience of conversion determined his concept of conversion. He thought of it as an instantaneous experience preceded by a long and hard struggle. He believed that a person should be able to recount the exact circumstances, time, and place of his conversion (Kuiper, p. 287).

Charles Haddon Spurgeon

Spurgeon gave his testimony of conversion as follows. "While under the concern of soul, I resolved that I would attend all the places of worship in the town where I lived in order that I might find out the way of salvation. I was willing to do anything and be anything if God would only forgive my sin. I set off, determined to go round to all the chapels, and did go to every place of worship, but for a long time, I went in vain. I do not, however, blame the ministers. One man preached Divine Sovereignty; I could hear him with pleasure, but what was that sublime truth to a poor sinner who wished to know what he must do to be saved? There was another admirable man who always preached about the law, but what was the use of ploughing up ground that needed to be sown? Another was a practical preacher. I heard him, but it was very much like a commanding officer teaching the maneuvers of war to a set of men without feet. What could I do? All his exhortations were lost on me. I knew it was said, 'Believe on the Lord Jesus Christ, and thou shalt be saved,' but I did not know what it was to believe on Christ.

"I sometimes think I might have been in darkness and despair until now had it not been for the goodness of God in sending a snowstorm, one Sunday morning, while I was going to a certain place of worship. When I could go no further, I turned down a side street and came to a little Primitive Methodist Chapel. In that chapel, there may have been a dozen or fifteen people. The minister did not come that morning; he was snowed up, I suppose. At last, a very thin-looking man, a shoemaker, or tailor, or something of that sort, went up into the pulpit to preach. Now, it is well that preachers should be instructed, but this man was really stupid. He was obliged to stick to his text for the simple reason that he had little else to say. The text was, 'Look unto me, and be ye saved, all the ends of the earth.' He did not even pronounce the words rightly, but that did not matter. There was, I thought, a glimpse of hope for me in that text. The preacher began thus: 'My dear friends, this is a very simple text indeed. It says, 'Look,' Now lookin' don't take a deal of pain. It ain't liftin' your foot or your finger; it is just, "Look." Well, a man needn't go to college to learn to look. You may be the biggest fool, and yet you can look. A man needn't be worth a thousand a year to be able to look.

Anyone can look; even a child can look. But the text says, "Look unto *Me.* " 'Ay!' said he, in broad Essex, 'many on ye are lookin' to yourselves, but it's no use lookin' there. You'll never find any comfort in yourselves. Some look to God the Father. No, look to Him by and by. Jesus Christ says, 'Look unto *Me.*' Some on ye say, 'We must wait for the Spirit's workin'.' You have no business with that just now. Look to *Christ.* The text says, 'Look unto *Me.*'

"Then the good man followed up his text in this way: 'Look unto Me; I am sweating great drops of blood. Look unto Me; I am hangin' on the cross. Look unto Me; I am dead and buried. Look unto Me; I rise again. Look unto Me; I ascend to Heaven. Look unto Me; I am sittin' at the Father's right hand. O poor sinner, look unto Me! Look unto Me!'

"When he had gone to about that length and managed to spin out ten minutes or so, he was at the end of his tether. Then he looked to me under the gallery, and I dare say, with so few present, he knew me to be a stranger. Just fixing his eyes on me, as if he knew all my heart, he said, 'Young man, you look very miserable.' Well, I did, but I had not been accustomed to having remarks made from the pulpit on my personal appearance before. However, it was a good blow, struck right home. He continued, 'and you will always be miserable—miserable in life, and miserable in death— If you don't obey my text; but if you obey now, this moment, you will be saved.' Then, lifting up his hands, he shouted, as only a Primitive Methodist could do, 'Young man, look to Jesus Christ. Look! Look! Look!' Oh! I looked until I could almost have looked my eyes away. There and then, the cloud was gone, the darkness had rolled away, and that moment I saw the sun, and I could have risen that instant, and sung with the most enthusiastic of them, of the precious blood of Christ, and the simple faith which looks alone to Him. Oh, that somebody had told me this before. 'Trust Christ, and you shall be saved'" (Spurgeon, pp. 86-88). Spurgeon was 15 years old when he was converted. He decided that day to preach the gospel (Day, p. 61).

R. A. Torrey

In 1871, at age 15, R. A. Torrey entered Yale, partly prompted by his mother, who knew of Yale's strong religious orientation. (Chapel was compulsive.) She was praying that her son might become a minister (Martin, p. 28). Although he had not yet become a Christian, he regularly attended church on Sunday, read his Bible, and prayed daily, habits that were ingrained in him from childhood. At the same time, he wrote, "In those days, I hated the Bible. I read it every day, but it was to me about the most stupid book I had read. I would rather have read last year's almanac any day than to have read the Bible…. In former days … I loved the card table, the theater, the dance, the horse race, the champagne supper, and I hated the prayer meeting and Sunday services" (Martin, p. 33).

Nevertheless, Torrey was still tormented by the thought that God was calling him to be a minister. At the end of his junior year at Yale, in the middle of the night, he woke up smothered with the feeling of deep despondency. In desperation, he jumped out of bed and opened the drawer, looking for a razor to end "this whole miserable business." At that moment, however, he dropped to his knees in the darkness beside the open drawer and began to pray. "God, if you will take away this awful burden, I will preach." Immediately, a strange peace settled over him; he went back to bed and fell into a restful sleep. Later, he remarked, "I'd gone to bed with no more thought of becoming a Christian than I had of jumping over the moon." He remembered that his mother, 427 miles away, was praying that he would become a minister of the gospel. He wrote, "I had gotten over sermons and arguments in churches and everything else; I could not get over my mother's prayers."

Roger Martin, Torrey's biographer, remarked, "The full realization of his conversion did not dawn upon him, as it is centered in his surrender to preach. And although there was no marked change in his life, nevertheless, he told his classmates of his decision. They thought he was joking…. It was not until the end of his senior year at Yale that he made a public profession of his faith and united with the church" (Martin, pp. 34-35).

J. R. Seely's book *Ecce Homo* convinced him to identify himself with the church. The book is not written according to Orthodox tradition. "Seeley stressed that a person had a valid title to citizenship in the kingdom of heaven if he were prepared to obey God and sacrifice something for Him. Entrance into the kingdom was by faith, but this was interpreted as the capability for better things. The author's further stress was that a person might legitimately become a Christian without a full and final belief in

Christ, and that progress in the things of Christ might be almost imperceptible. Ruben could readily assent to these propositions. Thus, his initial hesitation about uniting with the church because of his slow spiritual progress was overcome, and he decided to make an open confession of Christ" (Martin, p. 35).

Summary: The testimonies of the conversion of famous Christians and many today indicate that some explain their experience in biblical terms, while others do not.

Chapter 4

Conclusion

The text of Scripture is clear: salvation is by grace through faith, but Christians differ over the definition and content of "faith," and some testimonies of conversion by even famous Christians are "cloudy." How should we respond to the different definitions and testimonies that miss the mark?

Various Views of Faith

Mental Assent to a Proposition Granted, mental assent is involved in saving faith. After all, it is *believing* something. From a philosophical point of view, faith is indeed believing a *proposition*. From a biblical perspective, it would be better to say that faith is believing in a *promise* of eternal life. Using the word *promise* rather than *proposition* better conveys the idea of believing in a person *for* something. That is important. Saving faith is not just believing facts; it is believing in Jesus Christ, who died for our sins and rose from the dead, *for* the gift of eternal life [1 Tim. 1:16 NKJV, *for* the forgiveness of sins (Acts 10:43), *for* salvation (Acts 16:31), or to get me to heaven (Jn. 14:1-6)].

The critical issue is the word "for." Believing in Jesus is not believing in Him as a good teacher or example. It is believing in Him as the Son of God who died for sin and rose from the dead *for* the gift of eternal life.

Trust Both the Greek word and the Hebrew word for "believe" mean "trust." Adding the word "in" emphasizes trust. This definition of saving faith most satisfies the biblical data given in the previous chapter. Saving faith is trusting Jesus Christ, who died for our sins and rose from the dead *for* the gift of eternal life [Rom. 6:23; 1 Tim. 1:16 NKJV, *for* the forgiveness of sins (Acts 10:43), *for* salvation (Acts 16:31), or to get me to heaven (Jn. 14:1-6)].

In John 11, Jesus told Martha that He was the resurrection and the life and that all who *believed in* Him would have eternal life. Then, He asked her if she believed *that*. Martha affirmed that she believed He was the Christ, the Son of God. Hodges comments, "Thus, by believing the amazing facts about the person of Christ, Martha was *trusting* Him. She was placing her eternal destiny in His hands" (Hodges, *AF*, p. 39).

Today, using the word *trust* better communicates than using the word *believe*. After pointing out that Charles Hodge uses the word "trust," Ryrie says it "may be particularly appropriate today, for the words believe and faith sometimes seem to be watered down so that they may convey little more than knowing facts. Trust, however, implies reliance, commitment, and confidence in the object or truths that one is trusting" (Ryrie, *So Great Salvation*, p. 121).

Mental/Emotional/Volitional Those who preach that some people believe the gospel with their heads but not with their hearts and, therefore, are not saved, are preaching a man-made distinction not found in the Word of God. Robbins retorts, "No one will miss heaven by 12 inches, for there is no distance between the head of the heart: 'As a man thinks in his heart, so is he.' The head/heart contrast is a figment of modern secular psychology, not a doctrine of divine revelation. St. Sigmund, not St. John, controls the pulpit in all too many churches" (Robbins, in Clark, p. v). He also says, "Mindless encounters and meaningless relationships are not saving faith…. It is this pious anti-intellectualism that emphasizes encounter rather than information, emotion instead of understanding, 'personal' relationship rather than knowledge. But Christians, Paul wrote, have the mind of Christ. Our relationship with him is intellectual…. This recognition of the primacy of the intellect, the primacy of truth, is totally missing from contemporary theology" (Robbins, in Clark, p. vii).

Clark says that, in his opinion, "Many Christians, motivated by an irrational pragmatism or by an even more extreme irrational mysticism, consider belief to be an emotion or feeling. To be sure, some beliefs stir emotions, but the very sober belief that a man has five fingers on each hand is as much a belief as some shattering bad news. Nor can believing good news, namely the Good News, be a mere emotion" (Clark, p. 5). Clark also says, "That emotion sometimes accompanies volitional decisions cannot be denied; but this is far from insisting that an intellectual decision has emotion as a necessary ingredient" (Clark, p. 65).

Commitment The Greek word for "believe" is translated "commit" in John 2:24, where Jesus is said not to commit Himself to those who believed in His name when they saw the miracles that He did because He knew what was in them. If there is an element of commitment in saving faith, it is the commitment of one's eternal destiny to Jesus Christ. Ryrie says, "Of course, when one believes he commits to God. Commits what? His eternal destiny. That's the issue, not the years of his life on earth. Certainly, when one believes he bows to a superior person, to the most superior person in all the universe. So superior that he can remove sin" (Ryrie, *So Great Salvation*, p. 123).

Conclusion Saving faith can be expressed by saying, "I believe in Jesus Christ *for* eternal life." Or, "I am convinced that Jesus gives eternal life to those who believe He will give it to them." Or "I am trusting Jesus Christ *for* eternal life." Or, "I am trusting Jesus Christ, plus nothing, to get me to heaven." Or "I am trusting Jesus Christ for the forgiveness of sins." A person could also pray to Jesus *for* eternal life or the forgiveness of sins (Jn. 4:10), etc.

The Biblical Explanation

The biblical data indicate that faith involves being convinced that something is true (which presupposes prior knowledge of that something) and placing trust in it. In the case of salvation by faith, the faith is in Jesus Christ (Jn. 3:16; 6:47; Acts 16:31; etc.), a person. "The Bible certainly tells us that faith involves a person as its object" (Machen, p. 46). Abraham believed *in the Lord* (Gen.

15:6; Rom. 4:3). Paul said, "I know *whom* I have believed" (2 Tim. 1:12, italics added), not "what I believed." That means for people to be saved by grace through faith, they must *know* something about Jesus Christ, be *convinced* that something is true, and *trust* Him *for* something [*for* the gift of eternal life (Rom. 6:23; 1 Tim. 1:16 NKJV), *for* the forgiveness of sins (Acts 10:43), *for* salvation (Acts 16:31), or to get me to heaven (Jn. 14:1-6)]. What people need to know about Jesus Christ is that He is the Son of God, who died for sin and rose from the dead.

Testimonies

However, the testimonies of conversion, even of famous Christians, are sometimes anything but clear. Of all the passages in the book of Romans on justification by faith, the one Augustine landed on to be saved was Romans 13:13-14! Augustine wrote, "No orgies or drunkenness, no immorality or indecency, no fighting or jealousy. Take up the weapons of the Lord Jesus Christ, and stop giving attention to your sinful nature to satisfy its desires.' I had no wish to read more and no need to do so. For in an instant, as I came to the end of the sentence, it was as though the light of faith flooded into my heart and the darkness of doubt was dispelled." Wow! That passage in Romans was written to believers, not unbelievers. Moreover, if applied to sinners, it would be salvation by works! Yet no one doubts that Augustine was saved. R. A. Torrey testified that he was saved when he surrendered to preach. No one doubts his salvation either.

Clarks says, "Consider the case of Justin Martyr, one of the earliest heroes of the faith. Did he have saving faith? He was a Christian, was he not? He died for the name of our Lord and Savior. He must have been regenerated and justified, must he not? However, it is doubtful that any strong Lutheran or Calvinistic church would have admitted him even to communicant membership. His view of the Atonement was abysmal. Quite possibly, the strife-torn church in Corinth, troubled with fornication, lawsuits, and idol worship—its members do not seem to have denied Christ's resurrection, but they denied the resurrection of believers—had a better theology than Justin Martyr. But to what justifying propositions did he or they send? Justin Martyr was not a moron. Morons have doubtless been regenerated and justified. Some members of extremely primitive tribes also had incredibly confused minds. What propositions did they believe? Is there any passage of Scripture that identifies, in a scale of decreasing knowledge, the very minimum by which someone can still be justified?" Clark goes on to conclude, "The Bible commands the maximum, not the minimum (Clark, p. 109).

I have personally led people to Christ by telling them they must trust Jesus Christ, who died for their sins and rose from the dead, only later to have them say in a public testimony that they were saved when they asked Jesus into their hearts, an expression I did not use when I led them to Christ, but one they picked up because others were using it.

So, what must people know and be convinced of concerning Jesus Christ? Berkhof says, "It is impossible to determine with precision just how much knowledge is absolutely required in saving faith. If saving faith is acceptance of Christ as He is offered in the gospel, the question naturally arises, how much of the gospel must a man know to be saved? Or, to put it in the words of Dr. Machen: 'What, to put it baldly, what are the minimum requirements required, in order that a man may be a Christian?'" (Berkhof, p. 504, who says this is a perplexing question).

Could some people clearly understand who Jesus was and what He did, and that salvation was simply coming to Him for it, but use confusing language to express it? Is it possible that at the time of their conversion, people heard a clear message and definitely trusted Christ for salvation, but afterward were confused? Is that not what happened to the Galatians (Gal. 1:6-7)?

Personally, I have grappled with this issue since about 1960. In the 70s, in a lecture I gave at Dallas Seminary as an adjunct professor, which later became a chapter in the book *Evangelism: A Biblical Approach,* I spoke and wrote about using Revelation 3:20 as a salvation verse. After exegetically, contextually, and theologically demonstrating that "asking Jesus into your heart" is not a salvation verse, I concluded, "To crystallize and clarify even more, several observations need to be made. First of all, people are saved when a wrong verse or model is used. I am not saying, nor have I ever said, that people have not been saved when Revelation 3:20 was used. On the contrary, I think people have been saved when this verse was used, but in my opinion, that was in spite of the verse and not because of it. Augustine was saved when he read Romans 13:14. Does that mean we should use Romans 13:14 to lead people to Christ? I once met a lady who swore that she did not know anything else to do when she was saved, so she prayed the Lord's Prayer. Does that mean the Lord's Prayer should be used to lead people to Christ? Some people have heard and understood the gospel but have not trusted Christ. However, when they are confronted again and decide to come to Christ this time, they use the 'ask Jesus to come in' prayer. In their case, they grasped the essentials, and the words were almost immaterial.

"On the other hand, people have been deceived by this approach. I am personally convinced that many who have prayed to ask Jesus into their hearts were not regenerated. Because they were told that praying that prayer was the means of salvation, they thought they were saved. It would be much better to point people to Christ and the cross and exhort them to trust Him and His finished work.

"Once, another pastor and I were talking to a lady who said she was saved. The pastor asked her what she did to get saved, and she replied, 'I asked Jesus to come into my heart.' Not satisfied with that, he asked, 'If you were to stand before God and God were to ask you, Why should I let you into my heaven,' What would you say? Her response was, 'I love God and deserve it.' The more we talked, the more obvious it was that she had no comprehension of salvation and no relationship with Jesus Christ, but she thought she was saved because she asked Jesus to come into her heart" (Cocoris, *Evangelism: A Biblical Approach,* original edition, pp. 85-86; revised edition, p. 94).

Jesus said, "The one who comes to Me I will by no means cast out" (Jn. 6:37). As was pointed out earlier, in the Gospel of John, a number of different terms are used for faith, including asking

(Jn. 4:10), drinking water (Jn. 4:13-14), doing the good thing (Jn. 5:29), and working (Jn. 6:20-29). Jesus tells people to labor for eternal life (Jn. 6:27) but clarifies that the Son of Man *gives* eternal life, indicating it is a gift (Jn. 6:27). He says, "I am the bread of life. He who comes to Me shall never hunger, and he who believes in Me shall never thirst" (Jn. 6:35). Coming to Christ and believing in Him are synonymous in this statement, as are "never hungering and never thirsting" (Jn. 6:53). He says, "This is the bread which comes down from heaven, that one may eat of it and not die. I am the living bread that came down from heaven. If anyone eats of this bread, he will live forever; and the bread that I shall give is My flesh, which I shall give for the life of the world" (Jn. 6:50-51). He says, "Whoever eats My flesh and drinks My blood has eternal life, and I will raise him up at the last day" (Jn. 6:54). Jesus uses the figure of walking as a synonym for faith (Jn. 12:35), which is clear from the next verse (Jn. 12:36; see also Jn. 5:11). He even uses "following" as a synonym for faith (Jn. 10:27). The point is, whatever terminology is used, if a person understands who Christ is and that they are coming to Him for salvation, He will by no means cast them out.

This much is certain. We are commanded to preach the gospel (Mk. 16:15). The gospel is that Jesus Christ died for our sins and rose from the dead (1 Cor. 15:3-5). We are to tell people they are to trust Christ, the Son of God who died for sin and rose from the dead *for* the gift of eternal life (Rom. 6:23; 1 Tim. 1:16 NKJV; Jn. 3:16; etc.), *for* the forgiveness of sins (Acts 10:43), or *for* salvation (Acts 16:31). Our job is to communicate the message clearly;

God's job to give the increase (1 Cor. 3:6).

Also, when we encounter people who are not clear about the gospel, our job is to clarify the issue. "Now, a certain Jew named Apollos, born at Alexandria, an eloquent man *and* mighty in the Scriptures, came to Ephesus. This man had been instructed in the way of the Lord, and being fervent in spirit, he spoke and taught accurately the things of the Lord, though he knew only the baptism of John. So he began to speak boldly in the synagogue. When Aquila and Priscilla heard him, they took him aside and explained to him the way of God more accurately. And when he desired to cross to Achaia, the brethren wrote, exhorting the disciples to receive him; and when he arrived, he greatly helped those who had believed through grace; for he vigorously refuted the Jews publicly, showing from the Scriptures that Jesus is the Christ" (Acts 18:24-28).

Jesus commanded that the gospel be preached "to every creature" (Mk. 16:15), which by the nature of the case would require all believers to be involved one way or another. Like Paul, we have been "entrusted with the gospel" (1 Tim. 2:4). Our job is to clearly communicate that the faith required to enter heaven is trusting Jesus Christ, the Son of God, who died for our sins and rose from the dead, for the gift of eternal life, or justification, or for forgiveness and when we meet people who are confused about that to clarify the issues.

Appendix: GES View of The Saving Message

Grace Evangelical Society's (GES) explanation of what they call "the saving message" has evolved. As mentioned, GES was founded by Bob Wilkin, whose mentor was Zane Hodges. Over the years, as Hodges changed his views, Wilkin changed his to line up with Hodges.

For example, when Wilkin wrote his doctoral dissertation on repentance at Dallas Seminary, he concluded that repentance was a change of mind and it was required for salvation. Later, Hodges changed his mind. He concluded that repentance is not merely a change of mind, nor is it a prerequisite for receiving eternal life. His new view is that repentance is turning from sin and is required for harmony with God, meaning fellowship with God, not receiving eternal life. Even though Wilkin wrote his doctoral dissertation on repentance, concluding that repentance is a change of mind, he later changed his mind and accepted Hodges' new view of repentance. When Hodges modified his view on faith, Wilkin followed suit. In other words, on the subjects of repentance and faith, as well as many others, Wilkin's view, and, thus, the position of the Grace Evangelical Society, is Hodges' explanation.

My Connection

Before explaining Hodges' evolution, I would like to describe my connection with him. As a first-year student at Dallas Seminary in 1962, I took the first Greek class, taught by Zane Hodges. In that class, his theological views were never mentioned. It was the only class I had with him as the teacher. When I graduated from seminary (1966), I had no idea what Zane Hodges personally believed about anything.

From 1966 to 1974, I lived in Tennessee and traveled as an evangelist. During those years, having nothing to do with Zane Hodges, I rejected the critical view of the Greek text I had been taught in seminary and accepted the Byzantine text as superior. The man who changed my mind was John Burgon, who challenged the Westcott and Hort theory of the Greek text in the 19th century. In the process, I read Zane's article on the Greek text in *Bibliotheca Sacra*. In addition, I read his article on James 2 in *Bibliotheca Sacra*, which changed my mind about that passage.

In 1974, I moved to Dallas, Texas, to be an adjunct professor at Dallas Seminary. At that point in my life, I had questions about some passages of Scripture about perseverance, such as Hebrews 3:6 ("Whose house are we if we hold fast the confidence and the rejoicing of hope firm to the end"). Having heard that Zane had views on such subjects that would answer my questions, I went to see him. His explanation of that passage made more sense to me than anything else that I had ever heard. From that point, I did not hesitate to ask him numerous questions about various passages of Scripture.

In 1979, I became pastor of the Church of the Open Door in Los Angeles. As I preached through various books of the New Testament and encountered interpretive challenges, especially regarding the perseverance of the saints, I first formed my own opinion of what the passage taught and then sought Zane's view. When I went to Dallas for EvanTel board meetings, Zane invited me to preach at Victory Street Chapel.

During my week-long invitation to speak in the chapel at Dallas Seminary, a small group of students asked me to discuss Lordship Salvation with them. I invited Zane to that small meeting to ensure I had my Greek facts straight. His response was that he wanted to publish the lecture! I resisted, but he insisted. The lecture, *Lordship Salvation: Is It Biblical?*, was published by Redención Viva, a publishing company founded by Zane.

Zane asked me to read the manuscript of his book, *Absolutely Free*, before it was published. I met with him on two separate occasions (for a total of nine hours), trying to talk him out of including his new view of repentance and his view that genuine believers could lose their faith. As a result, he returned to Dallas and rewrote the chapter on repentance—making it stronger! I have since learned that Grace Evangelical Society board members tried to do the same thing, but, obviously, to no avail (Stegall, *The Gospel of Christ*, pp. 57-58).

The point is, I had a relationship with Zane Hodges. To this day, I deeply respect him, admire him, and, frankly, owe him a great deal. He taught me a lot, particularly pertaining to passages on perseverance and rewards. At the same time, I did not always accept everything he taught. Even before I rejected his new view on repentance, I did not accept all of his explanations, for example, his interpretation of the white horse in Revelation 6 (he thinks the white horse is Christ, not the Antichrist).

The Changes

Be all that as it may, Hodges' theological views have changed over the years. Wilkin has followed Hodges, and, thus, GES's positions have evolved.

The Gospel of John The Hodges/Wilkin/GES explanation of what they called the "saving message" is based on their interpretation of the Gospel of John. According to them, the Gospel of John is the only book in the Bible with the stated purpose of telling people how to have eternal life (Jn. 20:30-31). Since the Gospel of John does not mention the words "repentance" or the word "gospel" (Christ died for our sins and rose from the dead) and only mentions "forgiveness" in one passage, it is not necessary to repent or believe that Christ died for sin and rose from the dead to receive eternal life. Forgiveness is a fellowship issue, not an evangelistic issue.

Thus, the GES explanation of repentance, saving faith, the gospel, the expression "the Christ," and even forgiveness need to be examined, as well as topics such as the name of Jesus and the content of saving faith in the Old Testament.

Repentance: Hodges and Wilkin initially believed that repentance was a change of mind and was necessary for obtaining eternal life. Then, Hodges changed his mind. In his book, *Harmony with God* (henceforth HWG), he wrote, "I myself once held the 'change of mind' view of repentance and taught it" (Hodges, HWG, p. 11). His new view was that, instead of being a change of mind, repentance is a "decision to turn from sin" (Hodges, HWG, p. 58) and that it is not necessary to obtain eternal life.

Hodges concluded that repentance is not necessary to obtain eternal life because "the Gospel of John, which claims to be written to bring men to faith and eternal life (Jn. 20:30-31), never once even mentions repentance" (Hodges, HWG, p. 2) and "no text in the New Testament (not even Acts 11:18) makes *any direct connection* between repentance and eternal life. No text does that. Not so much as one!" (Hodges, HWG, p. 10, italics his). Therefore, he concluded, "Repentance is *not* a condition of eternal life" (Hodges, HWG, p. 3, italics his), and to say that repentance is necessary for eternal life is a "false premise" (Hodges, HWG, p. 11).

According to Hodges, instead of being a requirement for eternal life, repentance is "the call to enter into harmonious relations with God" (Hodges, AF, p. 145). "It addresses the need that sinners have (whether saved or unsaved) to repair the relationship to God in order to prevent or to terminate His temporal judgment on their sins" (Hodges, HWG, p. 49). In other words, repentance is connected to the forgiveness of sins (Lk. 24:47). Forgiveness is not a judicial issue; it is a personal issue, that is, *"personal harmony* between the offended party and the offender" (Hodges, HWG, p. 73, italic his).

In addition, when it comes to repentance, forgiveness, and baptism, the *Jewish believers in Palestine* were in a "special historical" situation. John the Baptist's message of "repentance for the remission (forgiveness) of sins" was to Palestine Jews and means that they "could not achieve harmony with God apart from receiving baptism. But it does not follow from this that forgiveness was bestowed at once on all who were baptized;" they still had to be born again by faith (Hodges, HWG, pp. 94-95). Nevertheless, "God insisted on this kind of baptism before He would forgive the sins of the believing Israelites or grant them the gift of the Holy Spirit (Hodges, HWG, p. 96). "Among *Palestinians*, God only bestowed the Holy Spirit on baptized believers (Hodges, HWG, p. 97, italics added).

Likewise, Paul is an example of salvation for *Palestinian Jews*. On the Damascus road, he believed and received eternal salvation. Yet Ananias told him that he had to be baptized to wash away his sins (Acts 22:16). After stating that, Hodges remarks, "Here we note again the eminent connection between baptism and the forgiveness of sins for *Palestinian* convert (even though he is in Damascus at that moment!)" (Hodges, HWG, p. 100, italics added). So, according to Hodges, Cornelius is "the classic model for *Gentile* salvation. He believed in Christ and immediately received the forgiveness of sins and the Holy Spirit (Hodges, HWG, p. 99, italics added), but because *Palestinians* were involved in the crucifixion of Christ (Hodges cites Mt. 27:25, HWG, p. 96), theirs was "a unique experience" that "can never be repeated" (Hodges, HWG, p. 105). They had to repent and be baptized before receiving the Holy Spirit, as explained in Acts 2:38, 8:12-17, 19:1-7, and 22:16 (Hodges, HWG, p. 106).

To sum up this view of repentance, 1) Repentance is not a change of mind; it is a decision to turn from sin. 2) Repentance is not required to obtain eternal life; it is necessary to have harmony with God, that is, fellowship with Him. 3) In the particular case of the Palestinian Jews, repentance and baptism were necessary to receive the Holy Spirit.

Saving Faith In *Absolutely Free,* Hodges taught that faith is *trusting* Jesus (Hodges, AF, 1989, p. 39). In *Harmony with God,* he says that the Jews in the book of Hebrews had "*trusted* in Christ alone" (Hodges, HWG, 2001, p. 121, italics added). Notice he used the word "trust" as late as 2001. Later, he decided that since the Bible uses the word "believe," it should be used instead of the word "trust," and he convinced Wilkin to do the same (Wilkin, "Trusting in Christ is Not Quite the Same as Believing in Him," GES Conference, March 1, 2006, cited by Stegall, p. 61). So, saving faith was changed from "trust" to "believe."

The Christ The GES "saving message" is that people must believe Jesus is the Christ (Jn. 20:31), which is believing He is the guarantor of eternal life (Jn, 11:27). According to Hodges, to obtain eternal life, all people must do is believe that Jesus is the guarantor of eternal life for all who believe in Him. He wrote, "If we believe that Jesus is the One who guarantees our eternal destiny, we have believed all we absolutely have to believe in order to be saved" (Hodges, "How to Lead People to Christ, Part 1: The Content of our Message," p. 5). To prove his point, he created an illustration focusing on two verses in the Gospel of John. He imagines an unsaved person, who knows nothing about Christianity, stranded on an uninhabited island in the middle of the Pacific Ocean. One day, a wet fragment of paper washes up on the beach. It contains the words of John 6:43-47, but all that is readable are the words: "Jesus therefore answered and said to them" (Jn. 6:43) and "most assuredly I say to you, he who believes in Me has everlasting life" (Jn. 6:47). Hodges contends that if this imaginary person *only* knew that someone named Jesus promised him eternal life and *he did not know anything else about this Jesus*, but he believed this Jesus guaranteed him eternal life, he would have it. He also cites John 3:16, 5:24, and Acts 16:31 (Hodges, "How To Lead People to Christ, Part 1: The Content of Our Message," p. 9).

But does the Gospel of John not say that people must believe that Jesus is the Christ, the Son of God, to have eternal life (Jn. 20:31)? The obvious answer is, "Yes." Hodges contends that believing Jesus is the Christ is nothing more than believing He is the guarantor of eternal life. His proof for that is John 11:27, which determines the meaning of John 20:31. In John 11:26, Jesus says to Martha, "Whoever lives and believes in Me shall never die. Do you believe this?" Instead of responding, "I believe that all who believe in You shall never die," Martha interprets Jesus' promise in verse 26 by saying, "I believe that You are the Christ, the Son of God, who is come into the world" (Jn. 11:27). Thus, Hodges says, "It is precisely the ability to guarantee eternal life that makes Him the Christ in the Johannine sense of that term"

(Hodges, "How to Lead People to Christ, Part 1: The Content of Our Message," p. 4).

To say that John 11:27 teaches that believing Jesus is the Christ is nothing more than to say that believing He is the guarantor of eternal life is to misinterpret the passage. For one thing, Martha said, "I believe that You are the Christ, the Son of God." Martha's answer includes more than just the fact that Jesus is the Christ; it also includes the fact that He is the Son of God. Hodges ignores that. Moreover, Jesus said, "I am the resurrection." Hodges does not include that. Based on this passage, it would be more accurate to say that to have eternal life, one must believe that Jesus is the Messiah, the Son of God, and the resurrection.

Hodges's new view means that Hodges changed his mind about believing the gospel. In *Absolutely Free,* he said saving faith is taking God at His Word in the *gospel* (Hodges, AF, p. 32). In *Harmony with God,* he wrote, "The Gospel of John is a presentation of *the simple gospel* of Jesus Christ" (Hodges, HWG, p. 110, italics his) and "Precisely because his focus on the core issue of the *gospel,* John has nothing to say either about repentance or about the subject of an individual experience of forgiveness" (Hodges, HWG, p. 111, italics added). The gospel, of course, is that Jesus died for our sins and rose from the dead (1 Cor. 15:3-5).

Later, Hodges concluded that eternal salvation was achieved by believing Jesus is the guarantor of eternal life, even without understanding that Jesus had died and risen. He says, "Neither explicitly nor implicitly does the Gospel of John teach that a person must understand the cross to be saved. It just does not teach this" and "God does not say to people, 'You trusted my Son's name, but you didn't believe in His virgin birth, or His substitutionary atonement, or His bodily resurrection, so your faith is not valid.' We say that, but God's word does not" (Hodges, "How to Lead People to Christ, Part 1: The Content of Our Message," pp. 7, 9). Hodges adds, "People are not saved by believing that Jesus died on the cross; they are saved by believing in Jesus for eternal life, or eternal salvation" (Hodges, "How to Lead People to Christ, Part 2: Our Invitation to Respond," p. 10).

Still later, Hodges went so far as to say that to require belief in Christ's deity, death for sin, and resurrection to be saved is on the level with Lordship Salvation, Roman Catholicism, the Jehovah's Witnesses, Mormonism, and Seventh Day Adventist (Hodges, "The Hydra's Other Head: Theological Legalism," *Grace in Focus*, September/October 2008, p. 2).

To summarize this view of saving faith, 1) Faith is believing, which is the word that should be used instead of trusting. 2) Saving Faith is believing that Jesus is the Christ. 3) In the Gospel of John, the expression "the Christ" means that Jesus is the guarantor of eternal life. 4) People can be saved without knowing the gospel, that is, that Jesus died and rose from the dead.

Oh, by the way, Hodges claims that saving faith involves assurance and eternal security (see https://www.youtube.com/watch?v=B8ZlkA4X5KI&t=1787s at 40:30–42:9). Nicknaming Hodge's view "the crossless gospel," Stegall said it is "completely unique to the Free Grace side of the salvation controversy" (Stegall, p. 35).

The Name of Jesus Hodges said, "Without the name of Jesus there is no salvation," … but "everyone who believes in that name for eternal salvation is saved, regardless of the blank spots or the flaws in their theology in other respects. Another way of saying the same thing is this: No one has ever trusted that name and been disappointed" (Hodges, "How To Lead People To Christ, Part 1: The Content of Our Message," pp. 9-10). In other words, all that is necessary to have eternal life is to believe in the name of Jesus, that is, that someone named Jesus guarantees eternal life.

Saving Faith in the OT GES teaches that the content of saving faith has remained the same since Adam, namely, believing that the Messiah is the guarantor of eternal life. Hodges says that Saul was saved by faith in the Messiah (Hodges, "Eternal Salvation in the Old Testament: The Salvation of Saul, in *The Grace Evangelical Society News*, 1994, p. 3). Wilkin concurs, "Eternal life has always been by faith in the Messiah whom God stands.... [Abraham believed in] the coming Messiah and Him alone for eternal life" (Wilkin, "Salvation before Calvary," *Grace in Focus*, 1998).

The Corrections

The Gospel of John To restrict the "saving message" to the Gospel of John and, then reduce it to a handful of verses in the Gospel of John (Jn. 3:16; 5:24; 6:47; etc.) is reductionism. Such an approach ignores the Great Commission, the book of Acts, and the epistles of Paul. See the chapter "The Explanation of Faith."

Repentance In the New Testament, repentance is a change of mind (see my book, *Repentance: The Most Misunderstood Word in the Bible*). Stegall points out, "If the term 'repent' means 'a decision to turn from sin,' as many crossless Free Grace people are now claiming, then this would be tautological in passages where the prepositional phrase 'from sin' or 'of sin' follows the command to repent (Acts 8:22; 2 Cor. 12:21; Heb. 6:1; Rev. 2:21-22; 9:20-21; 16:11). If the basic meaning of the word 'repent' consistently means 'to turn from sin,' then it would lead to the nonsensical redundancy '(turning from sin) from sin.' Therefore, a change of mind about the Lord Jesus Christ and the salvation He offers to undeserving sinners is inherent in the act of believing in Him (Luke 24:46-47; Acts 11:14-18; 20:21)" (Stegall, p. 59).

In a footnote, commenting on the Greek construction in Acts 20:21, Stegall says, "The two terms (faith, repentance) cannot be conceptually or soteriologically separated from each other as Hodges proposes. A person cannot have faith in Christ without having had a change of mind (repentance) toward God, any more than a person could have a Savior that is not God (Titus 2:13) or a predetermined plan of God that was not also foreseen by God (Acts 2:23), or a pastor given to a church by Christ who is not also a teacher (Eph. 4:11).... Repentance is inherent to believing though semantically distinguished from it.... Knowing is inherent to *believing* and inseparable from it, just as repentance is to faith.... Greek grammarian Daniel Wallace states, 'The evidence suggests that, in Luke's usage, saving faith *includes* repentance. In those texts which speak simply of faith, a 'theological shorthand' seems to be employed: Luke envisions repentance as the inceptive act of which the entire way may be called *pistis* [Greek: faith]. Thus, for Luke, conversion is not a two-step process, but one step, faith, but the candidate's faith that *includes* repentance'" (Stegall, p. 59 fn., italics his).

Repentance is necessary for salvation. According to Jesus, repentance and remission of sins are to be preached in His name "to *all nations*, beginning at Jerusalem" (Lk. 24:47; italics added). The Lord is "not willing that any should perish, but all should come to repentance" (2 Pet. 3:9). Even Hodges himself concedes that in the book of Revelation repentance is "clearly applied to the unsaved" (Hodges, HWG, p. 19) and in Luke 13:1-5, repentance is "addressed to an unsaved audience" (Hodges, HWG, p. 49; see also Nineveh, p. 50 and 2 Peter 3:9, p. 60). The objects of repentance in the New Testament for obtaining salvation are God (Acts 20:21), Christ (Acts 2:37-38), dead works (Heb. 6:1), and sin (Rev. 9:21; see Cocoris, *Evangelism: a Biblical Approach*, revised ed., pp. 72-73). In other words, people need to change their minds (repent) about works if they believe that works are what they need to be saved. When Hodges writes, "No one who believed in the worship of images was properly prepared to accept the exclusive claim of the Creator and His Son Jesus Christ" (Hodges, HWG, p. 85), is he not admitting that an idol worshiper must "repent" (change his mind) before he can be saved?

Saving Faith The word "believe" means to accept something as true and to trust (see the discussion of the definition of saving faith above). Stegall observes that the noun "faith" and the verb "believe" include the idea of "trust, reliance, or dependence." He adds in some passages, "'trust' is even the translation in many English Bibles (Matt. 27:23; Mark 10:24 [MT]; Luke 11:22; 16:11; 18:9; 2 Cor. 9:1; 1 Tim. 1:11; Heb. 2:13). There is no separate word for 'trust' in Greek beside the words normally translated 'believe' or 'faith,' or even at times, 'hope'" (Stegall, p. 61). He correctly insists that "trust" is a "valid synonym for faith" (Stegall, p. 64).

In the Gospel of John, believing includes more than just believing Jesus is the guarantee of eternal life. For example, in context, John 3:16 indicates that Jesus is the Son of Man (Jn. 3:13-14), that is, a human being, that Jesus is the Son of God (Jn. 3:16), that is, God the Son, that Jesus died for sin (Jn. 3:14), and that Jesus rose from the dead (see "who is in heaven" in Jn. 3:13). John 3:16 is not teaching the Jesus guarantees eternal life to those who believe in Him; in context, it is saying that Jesus the God/man, who died for sin and rose from the dead, gives eternal life to those who believe in Him.

When the other verses cited by Hodges are interpreted in their context, it becomes evident that none of them prove that all a person has to do is believe that Jesus guarantees eternal life to have it. They all indicate more about Jesus than that. Stegall shows that this is true concerning the context of John 5:24; 6:47; Acts 16:31 (Stegall, pp. 88-93).

Stegall shows the "absurdity" of Hodges' approach by imagining that instead of John 6:43-47 washing ashore, it was John 11:16-25 and that a portion of it was washed away so that what the maroon man found was a text that read, "Thomas, who is called the twin, said … to her, 'I am the resurrection and the life. He who believes in Me though he may die yet shall he live'" (Jn. 11:16a, 25). Stegall says, "Would God receive the sincere faith of the castaway and grant him eternal life if he innocently assumed the guarantor of eternal life was named 'Thomas' instead of 'Jesus'? Would the man's faith be disqualified just because he had the name wrong? You see, context is critical in determining the right content of our faith" (Stegall, p. 94).

I never thought I'd see the day when Zane Hodges would have to be told to pay attention to the context.

For a detailed discussion of the content of believe in the Gospel of John, see my book, *Believe in John's Gospel.*

According to passages outside the Gospel of John, saving faith is trusting Jesus Christ, who died for our sins and rose from the dead *for* the gift of eternal life [Rom. 6:23; 1 Tim. 1:16 NKJV, *for* the forgiveness of sins (Acts 10:43), *for* salvation (Acts 16:31), or to get to heaven (Jn. 14:1-6)].

To say that Jesus is "the Christ" is more than believing He is the guarantor of eternal life. According to Jesus, "the Christ" was "to suffer and to rise from the dead the third day" (Lk. 24:46). Paul thought that was the evangelistic message. In evangelistic situations, *it was his custom* to demonstrate from the Scriptures that "the Christ had to suffer and rise again from the dead" (Acts 17:3). The Gospel of John does not have a different definition of "the Christ" than Jesus and Paul. Taken as a whole, the Gospel of John clearly teaches that Jesus is "the Christ" (Jn. 1:41) and that He died and rose from the dead. Stegall maintains, "While it is certainly true that Jesus is *'the Christ, the Son of God,'* it establishes that Jesus is the guarantor of eternal life, the crossless interpretation of this key phrase seriously errs by reducing it to that meaning *alone*. It also creates more exegetical problems than it solves. For example, why would John have a special 'Johannine' definition of 'the Christ, the Son of God' that is completely unique to his gospel and distinct from all of the writers of Scripture? Also, why would John have a completely unique, distinctive meaning of the combined phrase 'the Christ, the Son of God' that the two individual parts, 'the Christ' and 'the Son of God,' do not have within his own gospel?" (Stegall, p. 71).

The Gospel of John may not contain the word "gospel," but taken in its entirety, it most assuredly presents the death and resurrection of Jesus Christ. In addition, the New Testament leaves no doubt that in evangelistic situations, the gospel was presented (Eph. 1:13; 2 Cor. 4:3-4; Acts 15:6; etc.).

To suggest that it is permissible to leave out the gospel (the death and resurrection of Jesus Christ) leads to dangerous practices. Antonio da Rosa writes, "If a JW hears me speak of Christ's deity and asks me about that, I will say, 'Let us agree to disagree about the subject.' I will discuss with him Jesus' ability to impart eternal life by faith alone apart from works. This is where I want to zero in with the JW or the Mormon. They believe that salvation comes by faith AND works, LOTS of works (not unsimilar to the Traditionalist religion). The moment that a JW or a Mormon is convinced Jesus Christ has given them unrevocable eternal life when they believe on Him for it, I will consider such a one saved, regardless of their varied misconceptions and beliefs about Jesus.... If someone asked me point-blank, do I believe that one must believe that Jesus is God in order to go to heaven, I would say 'NO!'" (Antonio da Rosa, cited Stegall, pp. 106-107). Did such people believe in "another Jesus" (2 Cor. 11:4)?

The Name of Jesus Five times the New Testament mentions "believe in His name" (Jn. 1:12; 2:23; 3:18; 1 Jn. 3:23; 5:13). In the Bible, a person's name does not merely distinguish one person from another. It is more than a label. It often indicates a person's prominent trait. "Adam called his wife's name Eve ("life") because she was the mother of all living" (Gen. 3:20). The Lord told Abram ("exalted father"), "Your name should be Abraham ("father of a multitude"); for I have made you a father of many nations" (Gen. 17:5). The Lord renamed Jacob ("heel-catcher") Israel ("Prince of God;" Gen. 32:28). Jesus gave Simon the name Cephas ("Peter"), which means rock (Jn. 1:42). The apostles gave Joseph the name Barnabas, which means "Son of Encouragement" (Acts 4:36). An Angel told Joseph to name the baby Jesus, "for He will save His people from their sins" (Mt, 1:21). The name "Jesus" means "Yahweh savings" or "Yahweh is salvation."

When it comes to believing in Jesus for eternal life, it's more complicated. For one thing, in the first century, "Jesus" was a popular name. Josephus, the first-century Jewish historian, mentions ten men named Jesus in the first century. In Christ's day, the name "Jesus" was found on a number of ossuaries (burial boxes) and tombs. It has been estimated that of among the approximately 80,000 men in Jerusalem during the first century,

7000 could have had the name "Jesus" and approximately 11,000 could have been called "Joseph," resulting in approximately 1000 males in Jerusalem called "Jesus, son of Joseph (Stegall, p. 136, see also fn.). According to Paul, people can believe in "another Jesus" (2 Cor. 11:4). So before people can believe in Jesus for eternal life, they need to know which Jesus to believe in, which is exactly what the New Testament repeatedly does.

For example, "God so loved the world that He gave His only begotten Son that whosoever believes in Him should not perish but have everlasting life." In just that verse, people are told that the One they are to believe in is the One God gave, which means the One God gave to die. In the context of John 3:16, even more information is given about this Jesus (see Jn. 3:13-15).

Acts 4:12 says, "There is no other name under heaven given among men by which we must be saved," but that verse is not teaching that all you need to know is the name "Jesus." Before Peter said that, he identified which Jesus he was talking about. He said, "By the name of Jesus Christ of Nazareth, whom you crucified, whom God raised from the dead, by Him this man stands before you whole" (Acts 4:10).

Saving Faith in the OT Dispensationalism teaches, "The basis of salvation in every age is the death of Christ; the *requirement* for salvation in every age is faith; the *object* of faith in every age is God; the *content* of faith changes in the various dispensations" (Ryrie, *Dispensationalism*, p. 115, italics his). Covenant theology contends that the content of faith is always the same. For example, Charles Hodge writes, "As the same Redeemer was revealed to them [people in the Old Testament] who is presented as the object of faith to us, it of necessity follows that the condition, or terms of salvation, was the same then as now. It was not mere faith or trust in God, or simply piety, which was required, but faith in the promised Redeemer, or faith in the promise of redemption through the Messiah" (Hodge, *Systematic Theology*, vol. 3, p. 96).

All who have accepted the GES teaching on salvation are dispensationalists, but on the subject of saving faith in the Old Testament, they agree with covenant theology. The issue is the content of saving faith. Perhaps a case can be made that people in the Old Testament were saved by faith in the coming Messiah (see, however, Isaiah 45:21-22), but the question is: "Did the content of faith change after the death and resurrection of Jesus Christ?" GES says the answer is "No." They argue that the apostles believed in Jesus as the Messiah without believing in His resurrection. That is true (Jn. 20:9), but after the death and resurrection of Christ, it became absolutely necessary to believe in the name of Jesus (Jn. 14:6; Acts 4:12), a concept the people in the Old Testament were not aware of. That alone proves that there's been a change since the death and resurrection of Christ.

Summary: Hodges and, consequently, Wilkin and GES, have revised their teachings on repentance, saving faith, the expression "the Christ, the Son of God," the gospel, forgiveness, the name of Jesus, and the content of saving faith in the Old Testament.

While I disagree with Hodges on critical issues about saving faith, he is making a point that deserves more attention. He says the temptation is "to test professions of faith in terms of doctrines we think must be believed. Instead, we should be focusing on whether an individual believes that Jesus has given him eternal life" (Hodges, "How to Lead People to Christ, Part 1," p. 8). He has a point. After all, it is possible to believe that Jesus died for sin and bodily rose from the dead and yet not trust Him for the gift of eternal life. Many Roman Catholics believe that Jesus died for sin and rose from the dead, but they do not trust Jesus and Him alone to get them to heaven. Hodges and GES make this point when they add the word "for" after the word "believed." They would say, "People must believe in Jesus *for* eternal life." (I would prefer to say, "People must *trust* Jesus for eternal life, that is, trust Jesus to get them to heaven.) Hodges says on a practical level, it is not only useful but "*essential* to explain that the Lord Jesus Christ bought our way to heaven by paying for all of our sins (Hodges, "How to Lead People to Christ, Part 1: The Content of Our Message," p. 12, italics added).

With all due respect to a man I admire as an individual and appreciate as an expositor on such biblical topics as perseverance and rewards, regarding the "saving message," Zane Hodges and his followers at GES have practiced reductionism and reinterpretation. Their explanation of the "saving message" has been limited to the Gospel of John; within it, it has been reduced to a handful of verses (Jn. 3:16; 5:24; 6:47; etc.). In the process, they have redefined words such as repentance, Christ, the gospel, and forgiveness.

Zane Hodges and his followers at GES limit the "saving message" to the Gospel of John because they say it is the only book in the Bible whose purpose is evangelistic. That is not exactly true. Read the purpose statement in John 20 carefully. It says, "And truly Jesus did many other signs in the presence of His disciples, which are not written in this book, but these are written that you may believe that Jesus is the Christ, the Son of God, and that believing you may have life in His name" (20:30-31). John did not say that the purpose of the entire Gospel of John was for people to believe that Jesus is the Christ, the Son of God, and that, by believing, they would have life in His name. He said that was the purpose of the "many other signs" Jesus did in the presence of his disciples. The seven signs of the Gospel of John are in chapters 2-12. The Upper Room Discourse, which begins in chapter 13, does not have an evangelistic purpose. Therefore, the purpose of the Gospel of John is more than giving an evangelistic message.

An explanation of the "saving message" should be based on the Great Commission, the gospel, the evangelistic sermons delivered by Peter and Paul in the book of Acts, the one example of an evangelist, Philip, leading somebody to Christ, and statements in the epistles.

In the Great Commission, Jesus commands the apostles to evangelize by preaching the gospel (Mk. 16:15), repentance (Lk. 24:47), and faith (Mk. 16:16). The gospel is that Christ died for our sins and rose from the dead (1 Cor. 15:3-5). In Acts, Peter preached the gospel (Acts 15:7). For example, in Acts 13:32, he said that he was declaring "glad tidings" (Greek: the gospel) to the people at the synagogue in Antioch Pisidia. He preached the humanity (Acts 13:23), the deity (Acts 13:34), death (Acts 13:28; see "the tree" in verse 29), and resurrection (Acts 13:30, 33-37). Paul did the same thing (Acts 17:2-3; 25:19; 26:22-23). Philip, the only evangelist in the New Testament, in his only recorded evangelistic message, preached about Jesus from Isaiah 53 (Acts 8:35), which includes the death and resurrection of Christ. Paul's evangelistic *custom* was to preach the death and resurrection of Christ (Acts 17:2-3; see also 14:7, 21). The *epistles* indicate that the gospel, the death and resurrection of Jesus Christ, was preached [Rom. 15:20; 1 Cor. 9:12, 15:1; 2 Cor. 4:3; Gal. 1:6-7; 3:1-2; Eph. 1:13; Phil. 1:12; 4:15; Col. 1:5; 1 Thess. 1:5; 2:9; 2 Thess. 2:14; Jas. 1:18, where "word of truth" is another name for the gospel (Eph. 1:13).

In other words, according to the command of Jesus, the examples of Peter, Paul, and Philip, and the epistles of Paul and James, to evangelize, we are to preach the gospel.

Ryrie wrote that the issue "is whether or not you believe that His death paid for all your sin and that by believing in Him, you have forgiveness and eternal life. Faith has an intellectual facet to it. The *essential facts* are that Christ died for our sins and rose from the dead (1 Corinthians 15:3-4; Romans 4:25)" (Ryrie, *So Great Salvation*, p. 119, italics added).

Here is an example of the way the gospel should be preached. "So what about you? Where do you look for peace and assurance of salvation? Are you asking, 'Have I done enough to prove I am saved?' Or is the question instead, 'Has Christ done enough on the cross to save me, whatever my faults and failures are or may become?' Does your entire hope for heaven rest on what *He has done* and *not at all* on what you can have or will do? If your answer to this last question is yes, then—clearly!—you have believed the Gospel and you already know that your eternal destiny is secure. Let it be said plainly: any system of doctrine that forbids us to find complete peace by simply looking to God Son, who was lifted up for us on the cross, can by no means claimed to be the true gospel" (Zane C. Hodges. *The Gospel Under Siege*, 2nd ed., Dallas: Kerugma, 1992, p. 150, italics his, cited by Stegall, p. 38).

Bibliography

Abbott-Smith, G. *A Manuel Greek Lexicon of the New Testament*. Edinburgh: T & T Clark, 1960 (reprint of the 1937 edition).

Alford, Henry. *The Greek New Testament*. Revised by Everett F. Harrison. Chicago: Moody Press, 1958.

Arndt, William and Gingrich, F. Wilbur, translated by Walter Bauer. *A Greek-English Lexicon of the New Testament and Other Early Christian Literature*. Chicago: The University of Chicago Press. 1979.

Bass, Clarence B. *Backgrounds to Dispensationalism*. Eugene, OR: Wipf and Stock, 2005.

Berkhof, L. *Systematic Theology*. Grand Rapids: Wm. B. Eerdmans Publishing Co., 1962.

Blum, Edwin A. "John." In *Bible Knowledge Commentary: New Testament*. Edited by John F. Walvoord and Roy B. Zuck. Wheaton: Scripture Press Publications, Victor Books, 1983.

Brown, Francis, Samuel Rolles Driver, and Charles Augustus Briggs. *A Hebrew and English* Lexicon *of the Old Testament*. Oxford: Clarendon, 1962.

Bruce, F. F. *The Epistle to the Hebrews*. New International Commentary on the New Testament series. Grand Rapids: Wm. B. Eerdmans Publishing Co., 1964.

__________ *The Gospel of John*. Grand Rapids: William B. Eerdmans Publishing Company, 1983.

Cairns, Earle E. *Christianity Through the Centuries*. Grand Rapids: Zondervan Publishing House, 1981 reprint (first printed in 1954; revised in 1967).

Cary, Phillip. *The History of Christian Theology,* Audio Lectures and Course Guidebook. Chantilly, Virginia: The Teaching Company, 2008.

Clark, Gordon H. *Faith and Saving Faith*. Jefferson, Maryland: the Trinity Foundation, 1983.

Cocoris, G. Michael. *Belief in John's Gospel*: *The Content of Believe in the Gospel of John*. Unpublished paper. Available at insightsontheword.com

_______________ *Evangelism: a Biblical Approach, first ed.* Chicago: Moody Press, 1984; *revised ed.* Santa Monica, CA, 2018.

_______________ *Lordship Salvation: Is It Biblical*? Dallas: Redencion Viva, 1983.

_______________ *Repentance: The Most Misunderstood Word in the Bible*. Santa Monica, CA.: J & M Publications, 2025.

_______________ *The Salvation Controversy*. Santa Monica, CA: J & M Publications, 2008.

Cole, R. A. *The Epistle of Paul to the Galatians*. 1965; rpt., Grand Rapids: Eerdmans, 1984.

Constable, Thomas, "Dr. Constable's Expository (Bible Study) Notes." Available at http://www.soniclight.com/constable/notes.htm.

Day, Richard E. *The Shadow of the Broad Brim*. Philadelphia: Judson Press, 1934.

Dods, Marcus. *The Expositor's Greek Testament.* Edited by William Robertson Nicoll. Grand Rapids, Michigan: Wm. B. Eerdmans Publishing Company, 1956.

Eadie, John. *Commentary on the Epistle of Paul to the Galatians.* Edinburgh: T. & T. Clark, 1884; reprint ed., Minneapolis: James and Klock Christian Publishing Co., 1977.

Erickson, Millard J. *Christian Theology.* Grand Rapids: Baker Book House, 1985.

Fung, Richard Y. K. *The Epistle to the Galatians* (The New International Commentary on the New Testament). Grand Rapids: Eerdmans Publishing Co., 1988.

Gonzàlez, Justo L. *The Story of Christianity.* Hendrickson: Peabody, Massachusetts, 1999.

Guthrie, Donald. *The Letter to the Hebrews: An Introduction and Commentary.* Tyndale New Testament Commentaries series. Leicester, England: InterVarsity Press, and Grand Rapids: Wm. B. Eerdmans Publishing Co., 1983.

Hodge, Charles. *Commentary on the Epistle to the Romans.* Grand Rapids: Wm. B. Eerdmans Publishing Co., 1967.

Hodges, Zane C. *Absolutely Free.* Grand Rapids: Zondervan Publishing House, 1989.

__________ "Eternal Salvation in the Old Testament: The Salvation of Saul, in *The Grace Evangelical Society New*s, 1994.

__________ *Harmony with God*: A Fresh Look at Repentance. Dallas: Redencion Viva, 2001.

__________ "How to Lead People to Christ, Part 1, *The Journal of the Grace Evangelical Society, Autumn* 2000.

__________ "How to Lead People to Christ, Part 2, *The Journal of the Grace Evangelical Society*, Spring 2001.

__________ *The Gospel Under Siege*, 2nd ed., Dallas: Kerugma, 1992.

Houghton, S. M. *Sketches from Church History.* Edinburgh, Scotland, UK; The Banner of Truth Trust, 2011.

Kent, Homer A., Jr. *The Epistle to the Hebrews*. Reprint ed. Grand Rapids: Baker Book House, 1983.

Kittel, Gerhard. *Theological Dictionary of the New Testament.* Trans. and ed. Geoffrey W. Bromiley. Grand Rapids: Eerdmans, 1968.

Kuiper, B. K. *The Church in History*. Grand Rapids: William B. Eerdmans Publishing Company, 1986.

Leupold, H. C. *Exposition of Genesis*, Grand Rapids: Baker Book House, 1963.

Liddell H. G. and Scott, *An Intermediate Greek-English Lexicon*. New York: Harper & Brothers Publishers, 1894.

Little, Paul E. *How to Give Away Your Faith*. Chicago: Inter-Varsity Press, 1966.

MacArthur, Jr., John F. *The Gospel According to Jesus*. Grand Rapids: Zondervan Publishing House, 1988.

Machen, Gresham J. *What is Faith*? Grand Rapids: Wm. B. Eerdmans Publishing Co., 1965.

Martin, Roger. *R. A. Torrey: Apostle of Certainty*. Murfreesboro, TN: Sword of the Lord Publishers, 1976.

Morris, Leon, *The Gospel According to John*. The New International Commentary on the New Testament. Grand Rapids: William B. Eerdmans Publishing Company, 1984.

Moulton, James Hope and Milligan, George. *The Vocabulary of the Greek Testament*. Grand Rapids: Wm. B. Eerdmans Publishing Company, 1972.

Parker, T. H. L. *John Calvin: A Biography*. Philadelphia: Westminster Press, 1975.

Ross, Allen P. "Genesis." In *The Bible Knowledge Commentary: Old Testament*, pp. 15-101. Edited by John F. Walvoord and Roy B. Zuck. Wheaton: Scripture Press Publications, Victor Books, 1985.

Ryrie, Charles C. *Basic Theology*. Wheaton, Illinois: Victor Books, 1986.

______________ *Dispensationalism*. Chicago: Moody Press, 1995.

______________. *So Great Salvation*. Wheaton, Illinois: Victor Books, 1989.

Stegall, Thomas L. *The Gospel of The Christ*. Milwaukee, Wisconsin: Grace Gospel Press, 2009.

Stott, John R.Stott. "Must Christ be Lord to be Savior? Yes." *Eternity*, September 1959.

Warfield, Benjamin Breckinridge. *Biblical Doctrine*. New York: Oxford University Press, 1929.

Westcott, Brooke Foss. *The Epistle to the Hebrews*. Reprint ed. Grand Rapids: Wm. B. Eerdmans Publishing Co., n.d.

Wilkin, Bob. "Salvation before Calvary." *Grace in Focus*, 1998.

About The Author

G. Michael Cocoris is a gifted communicator. He can make even complicated subjects simple, clear, and practical. His breadth of experience has allowed him to relate to a wide range of audiences.

Michael received a Bachelor of Arts degree from Tennessee Temple University, a Master of Theology degree from Dallas Seminary, and a Doctorate of Divinity from Biola University. He traveled the United States for over a dozen years as a speaker. He has also been a seminary professor, visiting lecturer, and world traveler, including hosting tours to Israel and China.

Michael has pastored three churches, including a rural church when he was in seminary, an urban church, the historic Church of the Open Door, first in downtown Los Angeles and later in Glendora, California, and a suburban church, the Lindley Church in Tarzana California, a suburb of Los Angeles. While at the Church of Open Door, he had a daily radio broadcast.

Michael has written numerous magazine articles, mainly for *Biblical Research Monthly*. He has authored a number of books, including *Seventy Years on Hope Street, A History of the Church of the Open Door*; *How To Live A Biblical Spiritual Life, Clarifying the Confusion; Repentance, The Most Misunderstood Word in the Bible; Evangelism: A Biblical Approach; The Salvation Controversy; Lordship Salvation: Is It Biblical?; The Books of the Bible, the Subject, Structure, Situation, and Significant Verses of Each Book; Psalms, A Song for Every Situation, Each Summarized on One Page; and Counseling Theories, A Biblical Evaluation.* In addition, he was a contributor to The *NKJV Study Bible* and *Nelson's New Illustrated Bible Commentary.*

Michael is the pastor of the Lindley Church in Tarzana, California. He and his wife, Patricia, live in Santa Monica, California.

www.ingramcontent.com/pod-product-compliance
Lightning Source LLC
Chambersburg PA
CBHW061749050726
47598CB00002B/657